DECODING VATICAN II

Interpretation and Ongoing Reception

CATHERINE E. CLIFFORD

2013 Madeleva Lecture in Spirituality

Paulist Press
New York / Mahwah, NJ

The Scripture quotations contained herein are from the New Revised Standard Version: Catholic Edition, Copyright © 1989 and 1993, by the Division of Christian Education of the National Council of the Churches of Christ in the United States of America. Used by permission. All rights reserved.

Cover and book design by Lynn Else

Copyright © 2014 by Catherine E. Clifford

Library of Congress Control Number: 2014936068

ISBN: 978-0-8091-4857-8 (paperback)
ISBN: 978-1-58768-331-2 (e-book)

Published by Paulist Press
997 Macarthur Boulevard
Mahwah, New Jersey 07430

www.paulistpress.com

Printed and bound in the
United States of America

Vatican II DECODING VATICAN II **DECODING VATICAN II** Decoding Vatican II DECODING VATICAN II **DECODING VATICAN II** Decoding Vatican II DECODING VATICAN II **DECODING VATICAN II** Decoding Vatican II DECODING VATICAN II **DECODING VATICAN II** Decoding Vatican II DECODING VATICAN II **DECODING VATICAN II** Decoding Vatican II DECODING VATICAN II **DECODING VATICAN II** Decoding Vatican II DECODING VATICAN II **DECODING VATICAN II** Decoding Vatican II DECODING VATICAN II **DECODING VATICAN II** Decoding Vatican II DECODING VATICAN II **DECODING VATICAN II** Decoding Vatican II DECODING VATICAN II **DECODING VATICAN II** Decoding Vatican II DECODING VATICAN II **DECODING VATICAN II** Decoding Vatican II DECODING VATICAN II **DECODING VATICAN II** Decoding Vatican II DECODING VATICAN II **DECODING VATICAN II** Decoding Vatican II DECODING VATICAN II **DECODING VATICAN II** Decoding Vatican II DECODING VATICAN II **DECODING VATICAN II** Decoding Vatican II DECODING VATICAN II **DECODING VATICAN II** Decoding Vatican II DECODING VATICAN II **DECODING VATICAN II** Decoding Vatican II DECODING VATICAN II **DECODING VATICAN II** Decoding Vatican II DECODING VATICAN II **DECODING VATICAN II** Decoding Vatican II DECODING VATICAN II **DE-**

CONTENTS

ACKNOWLEDGMENTS

I am deeply honored by the invitation to give the twenty-eighth Madeleva Lecture sponsored by the Center for Spirituality at Saint Mary's College and to join the company of distinguished women scholars who have contributed to this series over the years. Dr. Madeleva Wolff was a woman of foresight who, seventy years ago, opened the path to graduate studies in theology at Saint Mary's for religious and lay Catholic women. It was only in the late 1960s and 1970s that the first doctoral degrees in theology were awarded to women at other Catholic universities in North America.[1] I began undergraduate studies in the 1970s, intending to do a degree in social work, and enrolled in an optional theology course in the hope that I might come to a deeper understanding of my faith. I was drawn irresistibly to the sources of the Catholic tradition, and after two years, changed my major to religious studies. It took me some time, however, to discern that I was really called to doing theology as a vocation and a way of life. There were no women among my professors when I began my theological studies. Without women as models and mentors, it was difficult to find the courage to imagine embarking upon a scholarly vocation.

In the 1990s, after a long personal pilgrimage, I arrived at the Faculty of Theology at the University of St. Michael's College, Toronto, where I had the good fortune to meet Margaret O'Gara—a first-generation lay theologian. Margaret was an extraordinarily conscientious teacher with a rare gift of calling forth the very best in others and of treating others with the utmost respect. I absorbed a great deal from her about teaching and navigating the vagaries of university and ecclesial life. She became my thesis advisor and remained a discreet and steadfast presence in my life after graduation. I was privileged to work with Margaret as a colleague in circles of ecumenical dialogue and ecclesiological research. She served on the international Lutheran-Catholic Commission on Unity (1995–2006), on the Disciples of Christ–Roman Catholic International Commission (1983–2009), on the U.S. Lutheran–Roman Catholic dialogue (1998–2010), on the Canadian Anglican–Roman Catholic dialogue (1976–94), and took an active part in the meetings of Bridgefolk, a movement that brings together sacramentally minded Mennonites and peace-minded Catholics. In recent years, Margaret was instrumental in assisting the Canadian Conference of Catholic Bishops in its efforts to establish a formal conversation with representatives of the Evangelical Fellowship of Canada. As this very brief vita suggests, Margaret was the embodiment of the kind of dialogical engagement that the Second Vatican Council sought to instill in the life of all the baptized. Few others have taken more seriously the council's aim of promoting greater unity among the Christian churches.

Margaret was called home to God on August 16, 2012, at the age of sixty-five, after a two-year struggle with cancer. Her absence has made me—and no doubt many other colleagues and students—intensely aware of my indebtedness to her gentle mentoring and her example of prophetic leadership and service. An important part of Margaret's theological work was focused on the interpretation and reception of the First Vatican Council on questions of ecclesial authority[2] and on Vatican II's commitment to ecumenism. I wish to dedicate this monograph and my continuing work on the interpretation of the Second Vatican Council to the memory of Margaret O'Gara, in deep gratitude. I hope it might prove a valuable contribution to the reception of Vatican II's teaching in our time.

I wish to express my sincere appreciation to Kathleen Dolphin, PVBM, and the staff of the Center for Spirituality for their gracious hospitality during my stay at St. Mary's College. I greatly appreciate having had the opportunity to take part in a lively exchange with the thoughtful women who took part in the New Voices seminar. Our conversation has helped to inform and give shape to several elements of this monograph. Sister Kathleen is now retiring after many years of service to the Center for Spirituality, an important mark of which has been the caliber of the Madeleva series. Long may Saint Mary's continue to be a creative space where the voices of women are nurtured and celebrated.

Ottawa, October 2013

ABBREVIATIONS

AA	*Apostolicam Actuositatem*, Decree on the Apostolate of the Laity*
AG	*Ad Gentes*, Decree on the Missionary Activity of the Church
AS	*Acta synodalia sacrosancti Concilii Oecumenici Vaticani II*. 32 vols. (Vatican City: Typis Polyglottis Vaticanis, 1970–99)
CD	*Christus Dominus*, Decree on the Pastoral Office of Bishops in the Church
DH	*Dignitatis Humanae*, Declaration on Religious Freedom
DV	*Dei Verbum*, Dogmatic Constitution on Divine Revelation
GE	*Gravissimum Educationis*, Declaration on Christian Education
GS	*Gaudium et Spes*, Pastoral Constitution on the Church in the Modern World
IM	*Inter Mirifica*, Decree on the Mass Media
LG	*Lumen Gentium*, Dogmatic Constitution on the Church
NA	*Nostrae Aetate*, Decree on the Church's Relation to Non-Christian Religions

OE	*Orientalium Ecclesiarum*, Decree on the Eastern Catholic Churches
OT	*Optatum Totius*, Decree on Priestly Formation
PC	*Perfectae Caritatis*, Decree on the Adaptation and Renewal of Religious Life
PO	*Presbyterorum Ordinis*, Decree on the Ministry and Life of Priests
SC	*Sacrosanctum Concilium*, Constitution on the Sacred Liturgy
UR	*Unitatis Redintegratio*, Decree on Ecumenism

*Unless otherwise indicated, citations from the following sixteen documents of Vatican II are taken from Norman P. Tanner, ed., *Decrees of the Ecumenical Councils*, vol. II (Washington DC: Georgetown University Press, 1990), http://www.vatican.va/archive/hist_councils /ii_vatican_council/index.htm.

INTRODUCTION

Since October 11, 2012, we have begun to mark in earnest the fiftieth anniversary of the Second Vatican Council, a gathering of some 2,500 Catholic bishops from around the world who met each autumn in Rome over four sessions from 1962 to 1965. Vatican II is widely recognized today by scholars from across disciplines as the most significant event in the last century of religious history. Whether or not we are old enough to have experienced it—many of my undergraduate students were born a full thirty years after the close of the council—we have all been shaped by it, for the renewal of ecclesial life engendered by the Second Vatican Council has given Catholicism its contemporary form. Its consequences can be seen as well in the life of other Christian churches, many of whom sent official observers to the council sessions, and subsequently undertook a renewal of their ecclesial life on the model of the reforms undertaken by the Catholic Church.

Pope John XXIII set out two principal aims for this historic gathering. The first was to be the updating (*aggiornamento*) and renewal of the

Catholic Church. The second and related aim was the restoration of Christian unity. Vatican II would lay the theological foundations for a profound transformation not only of the inner life of the Catholic Church, but also of its relationships with other Christians, with other religious traditions, and with the modern world. In January 1963, an issue of *Time* magazine declared Pope John XXIII "Man of the Year" and observed: "[1962 marked] the beginning of a revolution in Christianity, the ancient faith whose 900 million adherents make it the world's largest religion.... Pope John XXIII...by convening...Vatican II set in motion ideas and forces that will affect not merely Roman Catholics, not only Christians, but the world's ever expanding population."[1] While this event would indeed have a profoundly transformative effect on the religious landscape, an adequate interpretation of the council and of the reforms that it set in motion must consider Vatican II as a religious response to change in the social and cultural world of the global human community.[2]

An ecumenical council is a privileged moment of communication or of proclaiming the faith of the church. Councils are perhaps the most effective way that Christians have found to discern the mind or the *sensus fidelium* of the whole church. An ecumenical council is a concentrated expression of the dynamic set of relationships that should characterize our living together as church at all times. In such a council, the entire college of bishops, who represent the local churches throughout the world, gathers to deliberate and exercise collectively their pastoral teaching office. Those councils that we designate as ecumenical are the occasion for an exercise of the highest instance of doctrinal authority and decision making in the life of the church.[3] As a gathering of bishops who preside over all the local churches, its ecumenicity is founded on the conviction that the gospel has been entrusted to the whole church. Because it expresses the faith of the whole church, an ecumenical council is the most authoritative teaching body in the church. The ecumenicity of the council derives from its representative character: the conciliar assembly represents and speaks to the whole church. In their role as teachers and judges of faith, the bishops in council give witness to the living faith of the whole communion of believers.

Each of the twenty-two councils that the Catholic tradition calls "ecumenical" has produced texts to summarize and communicate their decisions on matters of doctrine and church discipline. The Second Vatican Council produced sixteen documents. The corpus of these sixteen texts amounts to almost one third of the literature produced by all twenty-two ecumenical councils combined, or about half the volume of material produced by all previous ecumenical councils. This suggests, as John O'Malley has helpfully explained,[4] that the documents of Vatican II are something quite different from those produced by earlier councils. They are deliberately written in a very different literary genre or rhetorical style from previous council texts. Their very form suggests that we are dealing with doctrinal teaching in a new key.

For some, the reforms of the Second Vatican Council went too far. They may blame the council for the apparent decline of the Catholic Church in Western society and consider it a betrayal of tradition, a mistaken concession to modernity or to a world inherently hostile to all religious values. Others consider that the renewal of Vatican II was long overdue, yet did not go far enough. They see it as a well-intentioned, yet failed, project, stymied by institutional inertia or short-circuited by the resistance of an intransigent clerical caste. The reality of the conciliar event and the reception of the council's teaching are far more complex than either of these rather uncritical interpretations, which have been characterized as *traditionalist* and *progressive*, respectively.[5] Nonetheless, as we move away from the historical context of the council, it becomes more challenging to discern the enduring value of its teachings, to decipher their meaning and allow them to inform the life of the church in our own day. To do so, it will be particularly important to arrive at a proper understanding of the nature of the reform undertaken by Vatican II.

The reflection that follows explores some of the most significant challenges to interpreting the meaning of Vatican II in the present context, fifty years after the event of the council. The council itself provides us with some helpful clues to a correct reading of its teaching, contained in the sixteen documents of Vatican II and reflected broadly in the revised rites of the sacraments, in the revised Code of Canon Law, and in the numerous reforms to the structures of parish and diocesan life intended to support the life and mission of the church.

An examination of the council's own teaching reveals that at the Second Vatican Council, the Catholic Church came to a new consciousness of itself and of its responsibility in the world. Joseph Komonchak has written that Vatican II represents "an historic moment in the church's self-constitution and...an expression of the church's reflective self-consciousness."[6] That new self-consciousness is imprinted on every page of the council's teaching, a teaching imbued with a profound sense of agency in history. Underpinning that new sense of ecclesial self-identity is an associated recognition of the dignity of the human person and of all human persons in their diversity—a humble recognition of the cultural, religious, and ecclesial "other." A deeper self-consciousness of the church, its limits, and its nature as a participation in a constellation of relations of communion with others brought with it a conviction concerning the indispensability of dialogue. In the words of Yves Congar, the Catholic Church could no longer mistake "Romanicity" for "catholicity";[7] no longer take itself for the whole, or take its own social form as the only "legitimate" expression of human culture.[8] At Vatican II, the Catholic Church had to come to terms in an unprecedented way with the historicity of its expression of faith in a changing and increasingly pluralistic world. Mindful of the historical and social evolutions that have continued to shape the church in the fifty-year period that now separates us from the event, our task continues to be to distill the fundamental insights of Vatican II—insights into the gospel itself—that are still capable of guiding the life of the church in our day.

In the pages that remain, I hope to help readers "decode" some of the competing claims of our fragmented context and to propose a broader framework within which to consider the significance of Vatican II, a framework that can be distilled from a careful study of the history of the council and the documents it produced. Part I presents briefly the background to the recent polarization surrounding the interpretation of Vatican II, thus providing a context for understanding Pope Benedict XVI's reflections in 2005 on the need for a "hermeneutics of reform," one that takes seriously the historicity of church teaching and the contingency of ecclesial life. Part II surveys the wider discussion of Vatican II to distill several principles that might contribute to a responsible approach to interpreting the documents of Vatican II today. Continuing this discussion, Part III considers the extent to which a feminist hermeneutic might be applied to the conciliar teaching and provides an indication of the extent to which it is informed by the voices of women and women's experience. Part IV examines the history of the council and its teaching for clues as to how the council might be seen as a response to an epochal shift in human history, and one in which the Catholic Church experienced a new consciousness of its mission and responsibility in the world. Lastly, Part V explores how this new ecclesial consciousness is reflected in the council's commitment to enter into dialogue with other Christians, other religions, and science, culture, and the societies of the modern world. Commitment to dialogue is rooted in a deepened sense of the contingency of ecclesial life and is inseparable from the council's recognition of the need for humble self-examination and ongoing reform.[9]

Vatican II sought to reinterpret the gospel tradition and to rethink Catholic identity in the face of modernity. Its teaching points to an ecclesial consciousness irreversibly marked by a new sense of historicity, one that requires a shift in the hermeneutical task. The very event of the council itself and all of its teaching are a reflection of that new hermeneutic, a historically conscious effort to re-receive the tradition of the gospel for a new age. As this remains an enduring responsibility for Christians in every age, it is instructive to distill from the experience of Vatican II a number of principles capable of guiding the church today.

Part I

THE HERMENEUTICS
OF THE COUNCIL

Navigating Contemporary Debates

This book is concerned principally to explore the "hermeneutics" of the Second Vatican Council. To frame our discussion, it is helpful to begin with a brief word about the broad meaning of this term. *Hermeneutics* refers to the methods or principles for the interpretation of texts and of other forms of communication. The field of hermeneutics, much of which has been developed in relation to the exegesis of biblical texts or in philosophical reflections on human understanding,[1] often entails complex theories regarding the appropriate means for arriving at an accurate understanding of the meaning of a given text. Most contemporary discussion of hermeneutics will recognize that a text is inseparable from its author and its reader. Further, both the author and the reader are shaped by the context in which they write or receive the text. A word may have one meaning in a given social, historical, or cultural context, and a different meaning in another time and place. This poses challenges to the translation of a text and to the appropriation of its message in differing contexts.

The documents of Vatican II are mediators of meaning addressed to a community of faith. The farther we move away from the unique moment in history in which they were composed, the more challenging it becomes for us to interpret their message accurately. A correct interpretation must attend to more than their verbal content and form. A simple repetition of the content of the council texts cannot adequately convey their full meaning. Such an approach neglects the inevitable tensions evoked by the differing situations of authors and receivers, a reality that calls for a creative effort of transposition. To transpose the meaning of the council's teachings to a new context, it is helpful to consider what questions the council fathers sought to address. In so doing we can arrive at a better understanding of how and to what extent the methods or style of teaching adopted by Vatican II were shaped by the questions it sought to address. The council itself proposes a hermeneutic, an approach to interpreting the gospel tradition. We can learn from the originality of Vatican II's efforts to grapple with the questions of its day and find inspiration there to address new questions in our time.[2]

The distinctive style of Vatican II's teaching was in fact developed to take into account the receivers, to better communicate its teaching to modern men and women. Anyone wishing to interpret the meaning of those texts today must also take account of the fact that current receivers of Vatican II's teaching live in circumstances vastly different from that of the 1960s, when the documents were first disseminated. Thus, an important part of the effort to interpret the teachings of Vatican II in the present context involves a dialectic process of mediating between the cultural horizons of the council fathers and that of new generations of Catholics in the twenty-first century.[3]

A Polarized Context of Interpretation

When we begin to consider the dynamic interplay between texts, contexts, and receivers, or the differing emphases that some have chosen to place on one or other of these elements, we risk being drawn into a highly polarized debate that has surfaced and intensified over the past decade in relation to the scholarly study of Vatican II. At the heart of this debate are conflicting understandings of the relation of the teachings of Vatican II to the perennial message of the gospel and the tradition of faith. How is it that these texts communicate to us a message of faith that transcends the ages, and yet call for our creative response in each new age?

Just when the fiftieth anniversary of the Second Vatican Council might afford us an opportunity for a renewed study and reception of its teachings and insights, the pages of Catholic journals, magazines, and blogs have been cluttered with confusing claims regarding its significance and the reliability of certain historical and theological interpretations.

How is the average Catholic to make sense of these apparently competing narratives?[4] What are young Catholics—for whom Vatican II is largely unknown, or remains just another historical marker like Nicaea, Trent, or Vatican I—to make of the various characterizations of the council that want to pit the spirit against the letter, the text against the event, or continuity against discontinuity with the tradition? These heavily loaded terms have become an obscure code that now "complexifies" the interpretation of a teaching that we should be trying to make accessible to inquiring Catholics. No one disputes that Vatican II was a turning point in Catholic history. There is, however, serious disagreement concerning the evaluation or characterization of this change and its implications for the continuing life of the church.

Before we embark upon an examination of these debates, it is important to underline that the sixteen documents of Vatican II were approved by the council fathers with virtually unanimous support. During the actual deliberation and voting procedures, Pope Paul VI and the Council of Presidents[5] went to great lengths to obtain the broadest possible consensus for every text. In the case of the more contentious issues, the Council of Presidents provided opportunities to deliberate on the most controversial lines of the text line by line, seeking to obtain as much consensus as possible. Chapter 3 of the "Dogmatic Constitution on the Church," *Lumen Gentium*, which treats the much debated notion of episcopal collegiality, was the subject of more votes than any other council text: forty-one votes in all.[6] The largest number of votes against the final version of any single document was 164, or 7.7 percent, cast against a hastily dispatched "Decree on the Means of Social Communication," *Inter Mirifica*, in November of 1964. Opposition never amounted to more than 3.8 percent of the total votes cast for the remaining fifteen documents: 2,221 in favor, eighty-eight against, in the case of the "Declaration on the Church's Relation to Non-Christian Religions," *Nostra Aetate*. We should therefore be confident that the teachings of Vatican II received wide support among the bishops who attended the council, in marked contrast to the experience of the First Vatican Council, where a significant minority was poorly treated and opted not to participate in the voting of July 18, 1870, on the definition of papal infallibility. The documents of Vatican II stand as an extraordinary expression of the living communion of faith of the global Catholic Church. The virtual unanimity of the council's deliberations is important to keep in mind if we are to maintain a sense of proportion and of perspective when we consider the opposition being mounted today against many of the council's central teachings by a vehement traditionalist fringe.

During the proceedings of the council itself, a small but persistent force of resistance was embodied in a faction of the conciliar assembly known as the *Coetus Internationali Patrum* or the International Group of Bishops.[7] Its numbers varied according to the issues at hand, but a small core of the group was generally opposed to the entire direction of the council. Its opposition was epitomized in the figure of Archbishop Marcel Lefebvre, the Archbishop of Dakar and General Superior of the missionary Congregation of the Holy Spirit. He would reject the decisions taken to renew the life of the Spiritan religious order in accord with the principles of Vatican II at its chapter of 1968, and in 1970 founded the Society of Saint Pius X, the name of which is emblematic of all things antimodern.

In the early twentieth century, Pope Pius X mounted an aggressive campaign against the efforts of a disparate group of Catholic theologians who argued for the introduction of modern historical-critical approaches to the study of the Scriptures and of the Christian tradition. Suspicious of ideas emanating from the Enlightenment, including the notions of doctrinal development, separation of church and state, and religious liberty, Pius X condemned the works of several protagonists of so-called "Modernist" ideas.[8] He called for the establishment of Pian sodalities in every diocese whose task it was to rout out all danger of Modernist thought, and required all Catholic clergy to swear an antimodernist oath.[9] The latter practice was only rescinded in 1967. For Archbishop Lefebvre and other traditionalists, the teaching of Vatican II and the subsequent renewal of the face of Roman Catholicism contradicted the papally mandated principles of antimodernism, and thus marked an unacceptable departure from, or break with, the true tradition of the church.

A Rhetoric of Rupture

Lefebvre and many other members of the *Coetus Internationalis* understood tradition largely in terms of the ordinary teachings of the nineteenth- and early twentieth-century popes. For the majority of bishops at Vatican II, tradition had a much broader and more dynamic meaning. Many of the "new" developments in the doctrine proposed by the Second Vatican Council were in fact born out of an effort to reappropriate aspects of a more ancient tradition that had become obscured with the passing of time. The council's updating of the

church is inseparable from the theological movement of *ressourcement*, a return to the sources of
Sacred Scripture and the witness of the early
church.[10] Key conciliar developments—including
the pattern of the prayer of the church, an ecclesiology of communion that values the subsidiarity
and diversity of the local churches, the recovery of
an understanding of collegial character of the episcopal office and of the dignity of the baptized lay
faithful, and the recognition of the presence and
action of God's Spirit beyond the bounds of the
institutional church—are rooted in Scripture and
drawn from the sources of the first millennium.

Throughout the conciliar debate, Lefebvre
argued that the proposed documents, in particular
those on religious liberty, ecumenical and interreligious dialogue, and the church in the modern
world, represent a "new doctrine" and contradict
traditional teaching.[11] A similar perspective was
reflected in a letter addressed to Pope Paul VI in
1969 by Cardinal Alfredo Ottaviani, former
Prefect of the Holy Office and head of the
Doctrinal Commission at Vatican II, and Cardinal
Antonio Bacci, for many years the Vatican's principal Latinist, concerning the revised order of the
Roman Rite of the Mass prepared in accordance
with the directives of Vatican II's "Constitution on
the Sacred Liturgy," *Sacrosanctum Concilium*.
Complaining that the new order differed markedly
from the Tridentine liturgy, they argued that "The

pastoral reasons adduced to support such a serious *rupture*...do not seem to us sufficient."[12]

This letter was accompanied by a "theological study" of the Revised Roman Rite prepared under the direction of Archbishop Lefebvre. Cardinal Ottaviani later recanted his position after clarifications were provided by the Congregation for the Doctrine of the Faith. He regretted that the letter had been published at all, claiming he had not given his permission, but the damage was done. Lefebvre argued that following Vatican II Catholicism had evolved into a "new church," even a "schismatic church because it has broken with the original Catholic Church."[13] He considered the church of Vatican II as "neo-Protestant" and "neo-Modernist," and in his more polemical writings, embraced many ideas of the *sedevacantist* movement, contesting the authority of Pope Paul VI.[14] The notion of the council as a break, a rupture with the past, or as being in discontinuity with tradition is a leitmotif of traditionalist writings. It is important to note that "the rhetoric of rupture was already in operation during the council"[15] among those bishops who were sometimes characterized as *immobilisti*, a marginal group whose positions did not prevail.

The Canadian ecclesiologist and scholar of Vatican II Gilles Routhier contends that it is against the background of these traditionalist readings of the council that we must consider a series of statements that are emblematic of the orientations guiding the authoritative interpretation of the teachings of Vatican II at the highest levels. He names (1) the elaboration of the guidelines for interpreting the teaching of Vatican II by the Extraordinary Synod of 1985,[16] (2) the remarks of Cardinal Joseph Ratzinger in an extended interview given in that same year to Vittorio Messori and published in *The Ratzinger Report*,[17] and (3) the reflections of Pope Benedict XVI concerning the hermeneutics of the council given in an address to the Roman Curia on December 22, 2005.[18] Routhier writes that a close examination of these statements against the background of Cardinal Ratzinger's overriding concern to appease the traditionalist movement reveals the extent to which competing "ideological" and "political" interests have effectively "poisoned" and regrettably polarized or "politicized" discussions among historians and theologians concerning the interpretation of Vatican II and its enduring significance.[19]

This is a serious charge. It implies that for over three decades the official magisterium of the church has allowed its agenda for the global Catholic community to be inordinately influenced by the views of a minor fringe group. Further, it suggests that the authoritative reception of Vatican II has been skewed by a marginal faction of former Catholics who view themselves as a faithful remnant, and whose fidelity is conditioned by a staunch rejection of the council's teaching. It smacks of a schismatic tail wagging the magisterial dog. The focus of the debate on the interpretation of Vatican II has shifted from how to interpret a set of texts to how we understand the dynamics of tradition.[20]

THE EXTRAORDINARY SYNOD OF 1985

Among the criteria for interpreting the council put forward by the Extraordinary Synod of Bishops in 1985, we find the principle that "the council must be understood in continuity with the great tradition of the Church."[21] Soon after the election of Pope John Paul II in 1978, Archbishop Lefebvre adopted what appeared on the surface to be a more conciliatory tone than he had maintained in earlier exchanges with Pope Paul VI. In a series of negotiations brokered by Cardinal Joseph Ratzinger, he indicated that he would be open to accepting an interpretation of Vatican II "in light of the tradition."[22] The criterion of tradition, he argued, could provide a basis for determining which of the documents of Vatican II might be retained, and which might be corrected or simply rejected.[23] He stood by his contention that the council's teachings on religious liberty, on ecumenism, on other religions, and on the modern world were incompatible with the tradition. This codicil in the "Final Report" of the Extraordinary

Synod's directives for the proper interpretation of the Second Vatican Council was introduced into the text at the behest of Cardinal Ratzinger.

THE RATZINGER REPORT

Against the backdrop of his exchanges with the head of the Society of Saint Pius X, and reflecting on the challenge posed by the Lefebvrist movement, Cardinal Ratzinger insisted, in his famous interview with Messori:

> This schematism of a *before* and *after* in the history of the church, wholly unjustified by the documents of Vatican II, which do nothing but affirm the continuity of Catholicism, must be decidedly opposed. There is no "pre-" or "post-"conciliar church: there is but one, unique church that walks the path toward the Lord, ever deepening and ever better understanding the treasure of faith that he himself has entrusted to her. There are no leaps in history, there are no fractures, and there is no break in continuity. In no wise did the council intend to introduce a temporal dichotomy in the church.[24]

Note that Lefebvre and Ratzinger differ greatly in their understanding of the council's continuity with tradition. Pope Paul VI had earlier observed that Lefebvre's position was founded on a false understanding of tradition as a static, unchanging reality.

To make his case for the orthodoxy of Vatican II's teaching, Ratzinger insists on its continuity with the great tradition of the church. Yet in his effort to make constructive use of the notion of continuity, he would open the way, however unwittingly, to an interpretation of conciliar teaching that tends to minimize the newness of the council and its consequences for significant doctrinal development or structural and practical change.

The 2005 Christmas Address of Pope Benedict XVI

Soon after his election as Bishop of Rome, Joseph Ratzinger, now Pope Benedict XVI, reopened negotiations with the leadership of the Society of Pope Pius X, whose bishops—consecrated by Lefebvre against the express wishes of Pope John Paul II—had been formally excommunicated in 1988. In an address delivered to the Roman Curia in December 2005, he gave an extensive reflection on the correct interpretation of the Second Vatican Council, one that is far more nuanced than some have cared to notice. Many have incorrectly characterized Pope Benedict's 2005 Christmas address to the Roman Curia as juxtaposing a hermeneutic of continuity and a hermeneutic of discontinuity or rupture.[25] Some assumed that Pope Benedict's critical comments were aimed at the five-volume *History of*

Vatican II, written by an international team of scholars and edited by Giuseppe Alberigo.[26] Earlier in 2005, Cardinal Augustino Marchetto had launched a frontal attack on the Alberigo project in a book entitled *The Second Vatican Ecumenical Council: A Counterpoint for the History of the Council.*[27] Marchetto claimed that the Alberigo project places an undue emphasis on the conflicts experienced in the council debates and on the novelties of conciliar teaching. He suggested that the authors of the *History of Vatican II* set out to paint an image of an entirely new church, in discontinuity with the preconciliar one. His unfortunate misrepresentation of the Alberigo project was further supported by the efforts of Cardinal Camillo Ruini, Vicar for the diocese of Rome and President of the Italian conference of bishops, during a triumphal book launch for Marchetto in Rome.[28]

Both Marchetto and Ruini insisted on an interpretation of the council in serene continuity with all that went before, to the point of unduly minimizing any genuine development or newness. Marchetto and Ruini's foray into the discussion of the hermeneutics of the council was the occasion for Jesuit historian John O'Malley to pen his provocative and now famous essay, "Did Anything Happen at Vatican II?" An astute historian, O'Malley cut through to the heart of the problem raised by an undue emphasis on continuity, including the limits of the principles of interpretation advanced by the synod: "What is missing in the otherwise excellent norms provided by the 1985 synod is one that would read as follows: 'While always keeping in mind the fundamental continuity in the great tradition of the church, interpreters must take due account of how the council is discontinuous with previous practices, teachings, and traditions, indeed, discontinuous with previous councils.'" He argued that insisting on an excessive preoccupation with continuity "is to blind oneself to discontinuities, which is to blind oneself to change of any kind. And if there is not change, nothing happened."[29] In a similar vein, Stephen Schloesser, observing how necessary it was for the Catholic Church of the 1960s to change in the face of a changing world, was compelled to observe "how much purposeful forgetting—repression or amnesia—is required to make a case for continuity" as historians attempt to craft a new narrative of its history.[30]

Some took Pope Benedict's reflections on the hermeneutics of the council as support for an overly simplified hermeneutic of continuity. Attacks on the so-called Bologna School multiplied. Indeed, it became fashionable to accuse any theologian attempting to reflect critically on the teachings of Vatican II and their reception as promoting a "hermeneutic of discontinuity" in contrast to Pope Benedict's purported insistence on the necessity for a hermeneutic of continuity. A close reading of Alberigo's reflections on the council make it difficult to understand the reasons for such an inaccurate misrepresentation. In fact, Alberigo argued that the council represents a moment of "epochal change" in the life of the church that is synchronous with a transition in human history. He viewed the event of the council as a moment where the church moved from a "closed," "reductionist," and ecclesiocentric notion of Christian faith that had dominated since the time of the Council of Trent and was reinforced by the trauma of the French Revolution, to one deeply marked by the integration of a new appreciation of history and, indeed, of the historicity of the church and its teaching. It is instructive to consider his reflections in the light of Ratzinger's earlier comments:

But reductionism is precisely the danger that one runs in claiming that there is no "before" and "after" in the history of the church. A one-dimensional line may perhaps seem to be a sign of continuity, but it is, above all, a symptom of inertia and death, not of life. Concretely, Vatican II showed a profound and intense awareness of the unsuitability of many preconciliar tendencies when it came to expressing the *sensus fidei*. This awareness led the council—on some key points such as the concept of revelation, the mystery of the church, the relationship between the people of

God and the ecclesiastical hierarchy, *Romanità* as the mark of the church, the acceptance of Catholic ecumenism, and the vision of the church *in* history —to restore ties with the most authentic and earliest tradition, beyond the ad hoc formulations and controversialist approaches of the more recent centuries.[31]

Alberigo was critical of those who would minimize or deny the important developments that took place at Vatican II through an undue insistence on continuity. Nonetheless, he argued unmistakably for an interpretation of the Second Vatican Council that recognizes the consonance of the council's teaching with the broader tradition of the church. As a critical interpreter of the council, he did not gloss over its newness. This newness, he insisted, must be understood in the light of, and as a faithful reception of, the tradition.

A Hermeneutic of Reform

Beneath the debate on whether Vatican II is to be understood as being in continuity or discontinuity with the great tradition of the church is the question of change: What kind of change did the council seek to bring about in the life and teaching of the church? Pope Benedict's discourse provided some important elements for a response. He did not, in fact, juxtapose continuity and discontinuity in explaining his own position. In point of fact, he described a conflict between "a hermeneutic of discontinuity and rupture" and "a hermeneutic of reform in the continuity of the unique subject-church."[32] Where the former bears in it a propensity to divide the preconciliar church from the postconciliar, or to oppose the spirit of the council and the letter of the council texts, he argued that the latter—a hermeneutic of reform—is more apt to account for the complex nature of the council and its teaching.

To properly interpret the council, Pope Benedict argued, we must fully appreciate the historical moment that gave rise to its teaching. Simply put, he observed, "the council had to determine in a new way the relationship between the church and the modern era." He noted, in particular, "three circles of questions" that required a rethinking and a repositioning of the church: namely, the developments of modern science, the changing relationship of church and state, and the fact of religious pluralism. New developments in human history required that the church redefine its relationships to other Christians, to other religions, and to contemporary science, culture, and society. "The Second Vatican Council," he said, "with its new definition of the relationship between the faith of the Church and certain essential elements of modern thought, has reviewed or even corrected certain historical decisions, but in this apparent discontinuity it has actually preserved and deepened her inmost nature and true identity." Pope Benedict observed that a genuine hermeneutic of reform involves a complex "ensemble of continuity and discontinuity," and requires a balanced understanding of the historicity of the church and its teaching.

> In this process of newness in continuity, we have to learn to understand more concretely than heretofore that the decisions of the church in what concerns contingent facts—for example certain concrete forms of liberalism or liberal interpretations of the Bible—must necessarily themselves be contingent, precisely because they refer to a determined reality which is in itself changing. It is necessary to learn to recognize that, in such decisions, only the principles express the durable aspects, residing in the background and in motivating the decisions from the inside. On the other hand the concrete forms are not equally permanent; they depend on the historic situation and can, therefore, be subject to change. Thus, while the foundational decisions can remain valid, the forms of their application in new contexts can vary.[33]

The changing relationship between faith and science, Pope Benedict noted, includes the understanding of the place of historical-critical methods of biblical interpretation and their application to the church's teaching of faith. Though this point was not developed in detail, his discussion of the Council's teaching on religious freedom provided an important example of the role of a new historical consciousness in the elaboration of doctrine. The experience of the Second World War, in particular the genocide perpetrated against the Jews by the Nazi regime of Adolf Hitler, provoked a necessary rethinking of relationships between the church and Judaism, and indeed all religions. A new understanding of the potential dangers of a lack of critical distance between church and state required the embrace of the principle of religious freedom "to give a new definition to the relationship between the Church and the modern State that would make room impartially for citizens of various religions and ideologies."[34] Where the popes of the nineteenth century had opposed this principle—one that they associated with the violent overthrow of the privileged social location of Catholic authorities in European society—it now appeared as a "social and historical necessity" to guarantee the peaceful coexistence of peoples. Further, Pope Benedict argued that an adoption of the principle of religious freedom was required by a correct understanding of the relationship between faith and freedom: religious freedom is "an intrinsic consequence of the truth that cannot be externally imposed but that the person must adopt only through the process of conviction."

In making its own this principle of the modern secular state, one enshrined in the United Nations' "Declaration of Human Rights," Pope Benedict claimed that the Second Vatican Council has

"recovered the deepest patrimony of the Church."
Further, he maintained, "The martyrs of the early
Church died for their faith in that God who was
revealed in Jesus Christ, and for this very reason
they also died for freedom of conscience and the
freedom to profess one's own faith—a profession
that no State can impose but which, instead, can
only be claimed with God's grace in freedom of
conscience."[35] By revising its attitude toward modern thinking on this and other issues, Pope
Benedict contended, the Second Vatican Council
"has reviewed or even corrected certain historical
decisions, but in this apparent discontinuity it has
actually preserved and deepened her inmost nature
and true identity."[36] Where in the past the Catholic
Church had assumed a largely negative attitude
toward modernity, it has now committed itself to
a continuing dialogue with the modern world in
an effort to concretize its understanding of the
positive relationship between faith and reason.

Pope Benedict's case for interpreting the Second
Vatican Council as a moment of significant reform
in the life of the church makes it highly unlikely that
he was targeting the authors of *The History of
Vatican II* and more probable that his exhortation
against proponents of the rhetoric of discontinuity
were directed against those with more traditionalist
sympathies, including the Lefebvrists. What is
striking in these remarks is his insistence upon the
need to attend to the historical context of the

council's teaching, and to understand the historically conditioned character of previous expressions of doctrine and ecclesial life. Pope Benedict's comments suggest that we might consider Vatican II as a moment when the Catholic Church became more deeply conscious of both its contingency and its responsibility within the changing circumstances of history. The source for this hermeneutic of reform can be found, he told us, in the orientations provided by the opening remarks of Pope John XXIII and the closing remarks of Pope Paul VI at the inauguration and closing of the council, which we consider in greater detail in Part IV.

In July 2007, Pope Benedict relaxed the regulations for the use of the Tridentine Rite of the Eucharistic liturgy, once abrogated by Pope Paul VI, declaring that it "must be given due honour for its venerable and ancient usage."[37] In a letter to the bishops in which he sought to assuage fears that such a move would "detract from the authority of the Second Vatican Council," Pope Benedict indicated that his decision was a direct response to the heirs of Archbishop Lefebvre and others who mourned the loss of the baroque liturgy.[38] Then, in a surprising move, Pope Benedict lifted the excommunication of the Lefebvrist bishops in 2009, in a measure he hoped would lead to their eventual reconciliation and full reintegration within the Catholic Church—even though there had been no perceptible change in their position.[39] These

actions undertaken by Pope Benedict XVI in subsequent years gave credence, however unintention-
ally, to those who held that his true sympathies lay
with the proponents of the rhetoric of continuity,
and sought in his words a warrant for an
approach that would diminish the authority of the
council. His words and actions have been enthusi-
astically exploited by those who openly promote a
minimalist interpretation of the Second Vatican
Council and its teaching.

On February 11, 2013, Pope Benedict XVI
stunned the world when he announced that he was
no longer fit to fulfill the responsibilities incum-
bent upon him and resigned his papal office. His
successor, Pope Francis, has brought a new style to
the ministry of the Bishop of Rome. Reactions to
his humble style and stated intention of undertaking a new reform of ecclesial structures has been
somewhat mixed. Camps are somewhat divided
along many of the lines that have been outlined
above. While Pope Francis does not seem interested in reliving the debates of a council in which
he was not a participant, he continues to walk in
the fallout of the battle. The need for a responsible interpretation of Vatican II is no less important
today than it was before Pope Benedict left the
stage. The next part explores a number of guiding
principles developed from a broader perspective
for rereading the teaching of Vatican II for the
twentieth century.

Part II

PRINCIPLES OF INTERPRETATION

Stepping back from the competing narratives that have unduly polarized the context for recent studies of the Second Vatican Council, let us consider a wider framework within which one might responsibly arrive at a more balanced interpretation of the event of Vatican II and its doctrinal teaching. The notion of hermeneutics, as we saw at the beginning of part I, is most often understood as referring to the interpretation of texts, with particular attention to language and the meaning of the words. At a second level, hermeneutics is concerned with translation, not only translation into the vernacular of successive readers, but perhaps even more importantly when we are considering the effort of an ecumenical council, to give expression to the faith of the whole, to transpose that message into action. The notion of hermeneutics, from the Greek *hermēneia*, in the broadest sense and as it is frequently used by theological exegetes today, is concerned with the point of contact or the encounter between the text and the experience of contemporary people.[1] When applied to the interpretation of church teaching, this transposition becomes part of the traditioning process itself. Within that dynamic framework, we must continually ask ourselves how the council's teaching can continue to inform the life and practice of the church. An adequate understanding of hermeneutics will attend to these multiple levels of understanding, explaining, and appropriating the teachings contained within the documents of Vatican II.

First, we examine more closely the full scope of the principles for a proper interpretation of Vatican II described by the "Final Report" of the 1985 Extraordinary Synod of Bishops. This first set of principles might be seen as focussing primarily on the interpretation of the texts, in the sense of attempting to grasp their intellectual meaning. They center on the intertextuality of the sixteen conciliar documents, their pastoral and doctrinal significance, the relationship between the spirit and the letter of the text, and, finally, on the tension between the present context and a text formulated in the historical past. Second, we turn to a second level of interpretation or translation that is concerned to mediate, in a more intentional manner, between the world of the Second Vatican Council and that of the living community of faith in the present context. To carry out this task, we must be more alert to the world of the authors—including bishops, theologians, and observers—and of the whole church and the specific challenges it sought to address in the mid-twentieth century. We must also consider the specific literary genre and form of Vatican II's teaching, which provide an important clue to the intention of the authors. Finally, we turn to the receivers of the council's message both past and present. This final principle of interpretation points us to the importance of reception in the life of the church.

For an Understanding of the Texts

As we have seen in part I, a polemicizing discourse has focused almost exclusively on one principle of interpretation—continuity with tradition—almost to the exclusion of others. This narrow focus represents not only a failure to comprehend the nature of tradition, but reflects an undifferentiated consciousness, unable to distinguish between form and content, or between the appropriate requirements of gospel living from one historical context to the next. Pope Benedict's discussion of a hermeneutic of reform reflects a more differentiated approach and can be understood as being in harmony with the broader set of principles proposed by the Extraordinary Synod in 1985, to which we now turn. The actual teaching of the Synod encompasses a number of important principles, all of which must be taken into consideration in any responsible effort to interpret the documents of Vatican II:

> The theological interpretation of the conciliar doctrine must show attention to all the documents, in themselves, and in their close interrelationship, in such a way that the integral meaning of the council's affirmations—often very complex— might be understood and expressed. Special attention must be paid to the four major constitutions of the council, which contain the interpretive key for the other decrees and declarations. It is not licit to separate the pastoral character from the doctrinal vigor of the documents. In the same way, it is not legitimate to separate the spirit and the letter of the council. Moreover, the council must be understood in continuity with the great tradition of the church, and at the same time we must receive light from the council's own doctrine for today's church and the [people] of our time. The church is one and the same throughout all the councils.[2]

INTERTEXTUALITY

As these remarks of the "Final Report" indicate, any attempt to interpret the texts of Vatican II must recognize their intertextuality. No single document of the council's teaching can be considered in complete isolation from the others. For example, much of what is said regarding the specific vocations of bishops (*LG*, 18–27), priests (*LG*, 28), the laity (*LG*, 30–38), or religious (*LG*, 43–47) in the "Dogmatic Constitution on the Church," *Lumen Gentium*, is complemented by the particular "Decree on the Pastoral Office of Bishops," *Christus Dominus*; on the "Ministry and Life of Priests," *Presbyterorum Ordinis*; on the "Apostolate of the Laity," *Apostolicam Actuositatem*; and on the "Adaptation and Renewal of Religious Life," *Perfectae Caritatis*. Or again, *Lumen Gentium*'s understanding of the church as a communion of churches whose unity transcends a variety of liturgical, theological, spiritual, and canonical traditions (*LG*, 23) is reflected in the "Decree on the Eastern Catholic Churches," *Orientalium Ecclesiarum*.

Similarly, *Lumen Gentium*'s reflections on the relationship of the Catholic Church to other Christian communities (*LG*, 15) and to other religions (*LG*, 16) are further specified in the "Decree on Ecumenism," *Unitatis Redintegratio*, and the "Declaration on the Relation of the Church to Non-Christian Religions," *Nostra Aetate*. The "Declaration on Religious Freedom," *Dignitatis Humanae*, which recognizes the dignity of every person created in the image of God and affirms the freedom of conscience, provides an important clarification for the basis of the dialogue with others or for the appropriate conduct of evangelizing activity. Or again, the "Decree on the Missionary

Activity of the Church," *Ad Gentes*, cannot be considered in isolation from the council's reflection on contemporary questions developed in the "Pastoral Constitution on the Church in the Modern World," *Gaudium et Spes*.

The Eucharistic ecclesiology reflected in the "Constitution on the Sacred Liturgy," *Sacrosanctum Concilium* (*SC*, 41), is further developed in *Lumen Gentium*'s presentation of the particular church (*LG*, 23). Perhaps even more fundamentally, the conception of revelation as the personal communication of God's self in history outlined in the "Dogmatic Constitution on Divine Revelation," *Dei Verbum* (*DV*, 2), contributes to a dynamic notion of a living tradition that underpins the self-understanding of the church on every page of the council's teaching. The central themes of the council's teaching run like a thread through all the documents.[3]

It is important to be attentive to the structure of each document and to the relationship of each section to the others. By way of example, it must be noted that the doctrinal commission made a very deliberate choice to place chapter 2 of *Lumen Gentium* on the priestly people of God prior to chapter 3, which treats the role of the hierarchy. This ordering underlines the primacy of the share of all the baptized in the priestly office of Christ and of their call to holiness through the daily offering of their ordinary lives. Within this perspective, the ministry of the ordained appears more clearly as a service enabling the baptized faithful to live out their calling in the world. Similarly, the council's decision to include its reflections on Mary within the "Dogmatic Constitution on the Church" (*LG*, VIII) makes it clear that, rather than standing apart from or above the church, Mary stands firmly within the communion of saints as an image of faithful discipleship and a figure of the church (*LG*, 68).

As the synod suggests, there is also a certain "hierarchy" or priority of the documents that must be respected, a differentiation in the authority of the texts. The four constitutions—the "Constitution on the Sacred Liturgy," the "Dogmatic Constitution on the Church," the "Dogmatic Constitution on Divine Revelation," as well as the "Pastoral Constitution on the Church in the Modern World"—have a greater doctrinal authority than the associated decrees and declaration, and should therefore provide the overarching framework within which the others are to be understood.

Pastoral and Dogmatic Significance

Some are tempted to juxtapose the "Pastoral Constitution on the Church in the Modern World" with the dogmatic constitutions in an effort to downgrade its importance or to claim that it is of little or no doctrinal significance. Such

an approach, however, reflects a failure to understand that what is meant by the pastoral character
of the entire corpus of Vatican II—a point which
we develop more fully in part IV. Gilles Routhier
comments on the tendency of opponents of the
council to "promote the theory that the teaching
of Vatican II, in particular that of *Gaudium et
Spes*, does not have a permanent value due to its
pastoral character."[4] They claim, incorrectly, that
the council's teaching is so conditioned by the particular context and issues of the 1960s that it has
no enduring value or significance for subsequent
generations. Overplaying the card of historicity,
they take the pastoral character of Vatican II as a
pretext for claiming that its teaching is entirely cir-
cumstantial and of little relevance to the twenty-
first-century world.

An important footnote appended to the oft-
quoted opening paragraph of *Gaudium et Spes*
underscores the unity and interdependence of the
pastoral and doctrinal dimensions of the constitution. It affirms:

> The constitution is termed "pastoral" because,
> while it depends on principles of doctrine, its aim
> is to express the relationship between the church
> and world and people of today. As this pastoral
> aim is not absent from the first part, so the doc-
> trinal aim is not absent from the second....The
> constitution should therefore be interpreted

according to the general norms of theological interpretation and with due regard, especially in the second part [which concentrates on several aspects of the contemporary world], for the naturally changing circumstance of the matters treated.[5]

The alert reader, therefore, must be prepared to discern the doctrinal principles behind the discussion of their time-conditioned application in order to consider how they might best be transposed to the particularities of a new context.

This note also suggests that it is impossible to dissociate the doctrinal content from the pastoral form of style of the council's teaching. The doctrinal and pastoral aspects of its teaching are tightly interwoven and form a unity. The Belgian theologian Gérard Philips, Undersecretary of the doctrinal commission responsible for drafting some of the most significant conciliar texts, argued that the pastoral and doctrinal dimensions of the council's teaching were inseparable. Writing in 1963, during the first intercession, a determinative for the overall course of council, he observed, "The pastoral perspective is not something added on to the exposition of doctrine. It is inherent to that exposition, because the truth is essentially destined to be lived, and thus cannot be confined to a theoretical knowledge. This is why a separate treatment of doctrine and practice leads to a sort of vivisection that would be the death of the message's fruitfulness."[6]

Just twenty years after the close of Vatican II, the bishops of the Extraordinary Synod could observe that while the teaching of *Gaudium et Spes* had not diminished in importance, "the signs of our time are in part different from the time of the Council, with greater problems and anguish. Today, in fact, everywhere in the world we witness an increase in hunger, oppression, injustice and war, sufferings, terrorism and other forms of violence of every sort. This requires a new and more profound theological reflection in order to interpret these signs in the light of the Gospel."[7] As an example of how the times have changed, we might consider that with advances in technological warfare, the experience of war today is not what it was in the mid-twentieth century. In light of these developments, we might ask how the church's reflection on the principles of a just peace might need to be deepened. The synod affirms that new theological reflection must be informed at once by the council's teaching and by the new questions and insights of the day. The signs of the times that inspired the teachings of Vatican II may not be identical to the signs of the times that presented themselves to the church of the 1980s or of the present context. Nonetheless, the pastoral response and missional engagement of the church today continues to be informed by a deeper sounding of the great doctrinal tradition of the church carried forward by the teaching of Vatican II.

THE SPIRIT AND THE LETTER OF THE COUNCIL'S TEACHING

The "Final Report" of the 1985 Extraordinary Synod warns against a false understanding of the "spirit of Vatican II" as something that could be juxtaposed with the "letter" of the texts themselves or with the enduring authority of their teaching. Several years before the meeting of the Synod, Cardinal Joseph Ratzinger had already decried such attitudes. He wrote,

> An interpretation of the council that understands its dogmatic texts as mere preludes to an unattained conciliar spirit, that regards the whole as just a preparation for *Gaudium et Spes* and that looks upon the latter as just an unswerving course toward an ever greater union with what is called progress—such an interpretation is not only contrary to what the council fathers intended and meant, it has been reduced *ad absurdum* by the course of events.[8]

While the Synod is clear that the spirit of the council cannot be considered apart from the letter and the content of the council's teaching, it does not deny that there is a trajectory to be found in the council's teachings. A close examination of the council documents in their chronological order reveals a clear development and maturation in the formulation of conciliar teaching. This is one of the reasons why it is important to consider their inter-textuality, as we saw previously. While Cardinal Ratzinger seems to suggest that the council documents stand as a point beyond which an interpreter ought not to venture, it is clear that even the council does not claim to have spoken the final word on all matters. In a new context, we have still to carry out the task of discerning the enduring principles of which he has spoken and distinguishing them from the contingent form of conciliar teaching as we seek to receive it in our day.

If the teaching of Vatican II is to be truly received and inform the life of the church in each new context, it will not suffice merely to repeat the letter to the text. A real engagement with the documents involves striving to move beyond the surface of the text to embrace and appropriate the meaning they are intended to convey. German theologian Hermann Pottmeyer captures the interdependence of the spirit and the letter of the council's teaching when he writes: "Despite the limitation…of the conciliar texts, the 'spirit' of the council is tied to them, because without them it would lack any sense of direction. The 'spirit' of the council makes itself known from the direction given in the texts. Conversely, it is only in this 'spirit' that the texts are properly understood."[9]

To grasp the spirit of conciliar teaching, one must attend to more than the words on the page; one must also observe the structure and form of each document within the entire corpus of documents and place the whole body of teaching in historical context, within the broader horizon of tradition.

BETWEEN THE ORIGINATING TRADITION AND THE CHALLENGES OF THE PRESENT DAY

The final principle proposed by the Extraordinary Synod of Bishops points to the constant and creative tension within which the church will always live and in which any interpretation of church teaching inevitably takes place. The interpreter, like the ecclesial subject, abides between the originating event that gives rise to tradition and the contemporary world of meaning. Tradition is a reality that is not only rooted in the past, originating as it does in the history of God's revelation to humanity in the death and resurrection of Christ. Tradition is not simply a repetition or an empty echo of the past. It is not the mechanical transmission of a dead letter.

Tradition is a living reality, born through a personal and communal encounter in the present with the love of Christ, whose paschal mystery is actualized through the many experiences of compassion, mercy, forgiveness, and love that mark our ordinary lives. These are the realities symbolized in our celebration of Word and Sacraments and experienced in the fellowship of a living community of faith. The teaching of Vatican II stands as a mediator of the church's faith—the same faith that has inspired and informed the tradition handed down through the centuries from the first witnesses of the resurrection, and to which we are called to witness in the present context. Where the Second Vatican Council sought to translate the faith of the saints throughout the ages for the world of the mid-twentieth century, we are challenged to translate its message in creative fidelity for twenty-first-century believers.

The council documents, which are ultimately intended to be an authoritative mediation of the meaning of God's revelation to humanity in Jesus Christ, might bear within them what Paul Ricoeur has aptly called, a "surplus of meaning."[10] They may bear insights that go beyond even what the council fathers had anticipated, or be applicable to new situations in the life of the church and of the world that the council itself could not have foreseen. Readers of the documents of Vatican II who approach them from the perspective of a profoundly changed social and historical context might perceive new meanings or new applications of their teachings, exceeding at times what the council fathers themselves may have considered. Vatican II was itself an important instance of doctrinal development, the fruition of a long process of renewal in biblical, theological, and liturgical studies. The council might be considered a process of reappropriating the tradition. The reception of its teaching in a changing context may well create the conditions for recognizing the limitations of its teachings, but also for arriving at new insights that lead to further developments.

Mediating Meaning between the World of Vatican II and the Present Context

The brief reflection of the Extraordinary Synod of Bishops regarding the proper interpretation of the documents of Vatican II is focused primarily on the interpretation of the texts themselves. Scholars have generally agreed that a responsible and historically minded interpretation of the council texts must attend not only to the texts themselves, including the relationship of each document to the broader corpus of council documents, but also to their form and to the context in which they were produced, including the history of their elaboration and the intentions of the authors. These principles have long guided the interpretation of all ecclesiastical texts, including the importance of attempting to ascertain the mind of the authors whenever the meaning of a text is doubtful.[11] As we noted earlier, the form or style of Vatican II's teaching is quite unique in the history of conciliar texts. This rhetorical style was deliberately chosen in an effort to communicate more effectively to modern readers. Ormond Rush has observed that a sound interpretation of the documents of Vatican II must also take into account the "receivers" of the text.[12]

AUTHORS: THE WORLD OF THE COUNCIL FATHERS

To get at the meaning of the council's teaching, especially as we move away from the actual historical context of their elaboration, requires an effort on our part to enter into the world of the council fathers, their theologians, and of the whole Catholic community in mid-twentieth century in order to appreciate their worldview and their guiding concerns. Recent studies have begun to focus on the historiography of the texts as scholars gain access to new archival materials from the various commissions and subcommissions that drafted successive versions of each text. The *Acta*, or official acts of the council, provide us with access to the documents of the preparatory commissions, speeches of the council fathers, and their many written requests for amendments of the draft schemas.[13] As successive drafts were presented for the consideration of the bishops, each commission presented a *relatio*, or report, to the conciliar assembly providing a rationale and explication for important revisions. These sources are all important aids to those who wish to arrive at an accurate understanding of the meaning that the authors of the council documents sought to convey.

Many of those who took part in the Second Vatican Council—including bishops, theologians who served as *periti* on the various commissions, or as advisors to the bishops, ecumenical observers, and journalists—have left us a unique historical record in their personal accounts. They take the form of both published accounts and unpublished archival materials. Scholars have access to a vast body of literature generated by the actors themselves—more than perhaps any previous ecumenical council in the history of the church. This provides an unprecedented window into much of what occurred in the wings of the daily deliberations that took place in the general congregations within St. Peter's Basilica or in the workings of the various commissions. Theologians the likes of Yves Congar, Henri de Lubac, or Sebastian Tromp have left behind diaries and correspondence recording their impressions of daily meetings and often candid observations concerning the personalities and agendas at play in the very complex and human event constituted by the council.[14]

In the outworking of the council's agenda, we discover that bishops and theologians with differing, and at times, conflicting worldviews and inspired by differing theological perspectives came together to carry out the enormous task set before them by Pope John XXIII and carried forward by Pope Paul VI: to undertake a substantial renewal of the church, its teaching, and its structures in such a way as to enable the Catholic community to fulfill its mission more effectively in a changing world. Theirs was, in the most profound sense, a hermeneutical task, one of "reinterpreting the Catholic tradition in the light of contemporary challenges."[15] They were concerned to receive the rich heritage of revelation contained in the scriptures and in the tradition conveyed by the doctrinal and liturgical heritage of the church, all of which has its source in the divine disclosure of the love of God in the incarnation, death, and resurrection of Christ, and is continually enlivened by the power of God's Spirit in the lives of the living community of faith. Ormond Rush describes the task of the council fathers as one of *traditioning*, of handing on authoritatively the faith entrusted to the whole church, a calling at the heart of the church's responsibility from the time of Christ: "It had been from the beginning the mission of the church to tradition what it had received."[16]

It was this shared sense of responsibility for that transmission of the gospel tradition that impelled the bishops at the council to work toward a coherent consensus and common vision of the church and its mission in the modern world. As the continuing debate with proponents of a traditionalist perspective reveals, this posed a significant challenge even at the council itself. The most pointed contrast in perspectives emerged in discussions of the collegial nature of the episcopal office, in particular the understanding of the coresponsibility of the college of bishops in the governance of the universal church and its relationship to the Bishop of Rome.[17] Tensions became more pronounced when the bishops turned their attention to the relationship of the church to other Christian churches, to non-Christian religions, and to the modern world in the third and fourth sessions of the council.[18]

At issue were not only differing approaches to theology, but also the underlying issues of the relationship of the church to the world and its history. The synthesis of Catholic theology represented in the achievement of medieval Thomism, an approach that was rather uncritically revived at the end of the nineteenth century by Pope Leo XIII's *Aeterni Patris*,[19] no longer held sway in the face of renewed studies of scripture and theology. An ahistorical neo-Thomism proved an inadequate resource for answering the dramatic questions raised by early twentieth-century culture and history. The Dominican school of the Saulchoir led by Marie-Dominique Chenu and Yves Congar proposed a more historically minded approach to the Thomist tradition, still influenced by the realism of an Aristotelian worldview and its confidence in the capacity of the created world to serve as a mediator of God's grace.[20] Others, including

Henri de Lubac and Joseph Ratzinger, worked out of a more Augustinian tradition, one rooted in the idealism of Plato and less optimistic about the created world and the capabilities of human reason. As Ratzinger's comments on the spirit of the council would seem to suggest, these contrasting worldviews were perhaps most visibly at variance with one another in the elaboration and continuing interpretation of *Gaudium et Spes*.

However, the mind of the council fathers was not shaped only by fixed theological perspectives. They sought to discern the presence and action of God in history through their experience of the world around them. In his 1963 encyclical *Pacem in Terris*, John XXIII referred to this necessity of reading the "signs of the times," naming in particular movements in favor of workers' rights, of women's equality, and for the liberation of nations from the shackles of colonialism.[21] In their interactions with one another, the bishops at Vatican II were forced to recognize the rich diversity of experiences and perspectives represented by their fellow bishops who had gathered from the four corners of the earth and from the diverse churches of both East and West that make up the Catholic Communion of churches. Bishops from every region undertook a broad consultation of the laity, clergy, and religious of their local churches. The pooling together of these many voices—of the laity, of theologians, and bishops—was integral to the process of discerning the *sensus fidelium*, the consensus of faith in the whole church to which the council fathers would give voice.

In a manner never before witnessed in the history of the church, the bishops of Vatican II became mindful of belonging to what Karl Rahner has aptly called a "world church,"[22] one no longer coextensive with European civilization or centered in Rome, but now at home in a rich diversity of cultures and reflecting the complexity of the global human community. Former models of ecclesial self-understanding no longer held, and a new framework was required to express the identity of a rapidly evolving church. New forms of leadership and governance would be required to reflect the cultural diversity of this truly global community and ensure its unity. Indeed, never before had the question of the church been so central to the reflection and teaching of an ecumenical council. The decision to orient the teachings of Vatican II along the double axes of the life and nature of the church *ad intra* and the mission of the church *ad extra*, according to the plan presented by Cardinal Suenens in the final days of the first session,[23] is itself a manifestation of a new reflexive self-consciousness of the church and of this evolving sense of ecclesial identity.

The unprecedented form of Vatican II's doctrinal expression symbolizes what a number of scholars have referred to as the "style" of the council's teaching.[24] The Belgian theologian Joseph Famarée has aptly explained that the very style of the council's teaching is itself an interpretation of the gospel, a consciously chosen form of reappropriating the tradition. The decision to embrace this style was taken in the hope of making the message of the church's teaching more accessible to the receivers—contemporary men and women. A dialogical form was required to give expression to the pastoral intent of the council and its desire to become a church both engaging and engaged by others, in service of the human community.

No single author has given more attention to the question of the council's rhetorical style than the Jesuit historian John O'Malley. Indeed, O'Malley has gone so far as to declare Vatican II as the "Erasmian council," representing as it does the first time since the sixteenth century that the discourse of the church embraced the high ideals of the humanist tradition upheld by the Renaissance, namely, the principles of social commitment, human dignity, freedom of conscience, and respectful dialogue.[25] In contrast to the strident and often polemical style that increasingly marked the theological debates of the sixteenth century, Erasmus of Rotterdam preferred a more moderate tone.

O'Malley observes that previous ecumenical councils understood themselves primarily as legislative events. Their preferred style of discourse is assertive, opting for the form of short, blunt declarations.

> They made laws, and they rendered verdicts of guilty or not guilty. Neither of those two kinds of pronouncements are invitations to dialogue. They assert. In their canons, which were short ordinances and were the councils' most characteristic form of discourse, they lay down the law. The formula goes this way: "If anybody should say such and such, let him be anathema." "If anybody should do such and such, let him be anathema." Out you go! No discussion![26]

"As a form of religious discourse," he observes, "dialogue would not return until the twentieth century."[27] Vatican II moves away from these declarative "I-say-unto-you" statements to adopt a rhetorical style modeled on the great Greco-Roman classics and the writings of the church fathers. Its language and style is one of persuasion. Its teaching seeks to invite rather than deter, affirming rather than condemning. The rhetorical style that distinguishes the documents of the Second Vatican Council from previous conciliar teaching reflects a conscious effort to sketch out an ideal of gospel living that will inspire and motivate the receivers to respond in faith and action.

Receivers of the Council's Teaching

More than any previous council, Vatican II addressed itself to ordinary believers. Indeed, *Gaudium et Spes* is addressed to all people of good will. While some authors suggest that the rising importance of mass communication may have been a factor in influencing the council's desire to communicate more effectively with the wider ecclesial and human community, to my knowledge, none has recognized the role played by the advance in levels of literacy. Previous ecumenical councils were most often addressed to other bishops, clergy, sovereigns, and magistrates—the literate classes of society. It was not expected that the common people would have any interest in reading their judgments and declarations. In the twentieth century, however, levels of literacy increased dramatically.

Yet the decision to opt for a more engaging style of rhetoric should not be seen merely as a strategy for communication, or—as we might be tempted to consider in twenty-first-century terms—an effort to do a better job of marketing Catholicism's "brand." The bishops of Vatican II brought with them a heightened sense of the coresponsibility of all the baptized for the life and mission of the church. In their daily ministry, they had experienced a real collaboration in mission with all the faithful. They could no longer imagine teaching "over their heads," as it were. Many leading figures on the commissions responsible for drafting the council texts had a long experience of working with lay movements such as Catholic Action. They were acutely aware of how closely the activities of the council were being followed by well-informed Catholics around the world and were thus aware of the significance of communicating the council's teaching in an engaging manner. They sought to address ordinary Christians and speak to the many pressing concerns they experienced each day in family life, in the workplace, and in the economic sphere, taking their cue from Pope John XXIII, who, in his opening address to the council fathers, *Gaudet Mater Ecclesia*, called on the bishops "to make use of the medicine of mercy rather than that of severity."[28]

Vatican II's attention to the receivers of church teaching might also be considered a reflection of a deeper awareness of the sense of the faithful or the *sensus fidelium*. In his nineteenth-century studies on the role of the lay faithful in the life and teaching of the church, John Henry Newman drew the attention of theologians to this theological concept that had been largely lost from view.[29] The theological notion of the *sensus fidelium* expresses the idea that God's self-revelation in Jesus Christ has been entrusted to the whole community of the baptized faithful, all of whom share responsibility for the handing on of the gospel message—each according to his or her gifts. This common participation in the prophetic role of Christ is evident whenever they "render him a living witness, especially through a life of faith and charity, and when [they] offer to God a sacrifice of praise" (*LG*, 12).

The "Dogmatic Constitution on the Church," echoing Augustine, links this common sense of faith to the church's charism of infallibility that is manifested whenever "'from the bishops down to the last of the faithful laity' it expresses the consent of all in faith and morals" (*LG*, 12). The consensus of the faithful is important for discerning the faith of the whole church in the process of teaching. Their common reception is an integral dimension of that process.[30] In the reception of church teaching, the people of God say their "Amen," a word of recognition that arises spontaneously in the hearts of those who earnestly strive to live in fidelity to the faith handed on to us from the first apostolic witnesses.[31]

This thumbnail sketch of principles for interpreting the documents of the Second Vatican Council should make it clear that there is great need today for both critical and historical studies on the event of the council and its subsequent reception if we are to discern its enduring value for our times. To carry forward the tasks of understanding, interpreting, and appropriating the teaching of Vatican II, we must be committed to forming both scholars and pastoral leaders equipped with the knowledge and skills to accomplish the immense undertaking of forming new generations of Catholics who are sufficiently literate in the knowledge of the scriptures and of the church's teachings to live by them. Among the interpreters of Vatican II's teachings in our day is a new generation of women theologians and ecclesial ministers who now play an important role in faithfully interpreting the teaching of the gospel to others. In the next part, we examine how the perspectives of women have influenced the teaching of the council and continue to shape its interpretation.

Part III

A FEMINIST HERMENEUTIC OF VATICAN II?

I regularly teach a course in ecclesiology in which students are introduced to the self-understanding of the church reflected in the documents of Vatican II. Every year students ask whether the course will have a separate chapter on women in the church, hoping to hear what the council has to say about women. When I point out that there is no point in the council's teaching at which women are the object of a sustained reflection or are treated as a distinct group of persons within the community of all the baptized, some are tempted to conclude that the council may have forgotten women, or that women had no part to play in either the event of the council or in the elaboration of its teaching. The relative silence of the council on the question of women, seen through a hermeneutic of suspicion, might be taken to mean that women had no voice at all. Yet this would be inaccurate. Although women may not have been center stage at Vatican II and they are not the focal point of the council's teaching, their influence on the council documents was not negligible. In the context of the 1960s, Vatican II's repeated and unambiguous affirmation of the dignity and equality of women in church in society marked a great stride forward.

A second, related question, and one that is appropriate to ask in the context of the Madeleva series, is whether any systematic reflection has been carried out to date to provide a feminist reading or interpretation of the documents of Vatican II. The Second Vatican Council was contemporaneous with the first signs of second-wave feminism signaled by the publication of Betty Friedan's *Feminine Mystique*[1] in 1963. Since the time of the council, we have witnessed the emergence of contextual and liberation theologies that take seriously the experience of the oppressed. They seek to bring forward the forgotten voices of the poor, the exploited, and the dispossessed. Among these movements is that of Christian feminist theology, which challenges the predominance of patriarchy and the influence of sexism in the Christian tradition. It critiques the practice of valuing men over women, of taking men's experience as normative, of using masculine metaphors to the exclusion of feminine images in speech about God, and deplores the use of so-called Christian teaching to promote violence against women. Feminist theologies bring forward the voices and perspectives of women in order to promote the equal dignity and full participation in the life of the church and society.

To my knowledge, a systematic feminist reading of Vatican II's teaching has yet to be fully developed. Rosemary Radford Reuther's *Woman Church*, written in 1986, treats the development of alternate liturgical communities created in reaction to the patriarchy of the churches that excludes women's experience. Elisabeth Schüssler Fiorenza's pioneering works *A Discipleship of Equals* and *In Memory of Her*,[2] published in 1993 and 1994, respectively, explore the early tradition to recover an understanding of the role of women in the early Christian community. In that same period, the Reformed theologian Letty M. Russell provided a feminist interpretation of the contemporary church in *Church in the Round*.[3] Russell's dialogue partners included the Faith and Order Commission of the World Council of Churches and many other theologians, Catholics among them. However, she did not treat the documents of Vatican II in a systematic way.

Massimo Faggioli views the work of Catholic feminist theologians and other forms of contextual and liberation theology as a consequence of the "hermeneutical shift" that occurred at the council.[4] He suggested that Catholic feminist scholars such as Anne Carr and Elizabeth Johnson have taken Vatican II as a starting point rather than as the focus or end point of their theology. While their work attends to the experience of women in the church, it can also extend to include political, economic, and cultural concerns within a broad network of ecumenical and interreligious relationships. Elizabeth Schüssler Fiorenza exemplified a feminist extrapolation of Vatican II's perspectives when she wrote that movements of theological renewal

> have attempted to overturn monarchic, exclusivist, and fundamentalist pre-Vatican II church into a church that would respect religious liberty, privilege the "option for the poor," and strive to reform Catholicism in light of the radical democratic vision of the people of G*d. Although the Second Vatican Council did not specifically wrestle with the problem of women, the ekklesial status of women is the linchpin for any such social and ekklesial reform program.[5]

Freeing Theology is a collection of essays by leading Catholic feminist scholars that provides an overview of the contributions of feminist thought to central questions in Catholic theology. Mary E. Hines proposed a reflection on Catholic ecclesiology seeking to expand the council's understanding of the church as a communion of equals as a basis for advancing feminist concerns and for promoting the community of women and men in the church.[6] Mary Catherine Hilkert reflected on how Vatican II's theology of revelation opened the way to rethinking the role of experience in the divine human encounter. She noted that women's experience is not always adequately reflected in models of revelation or in women's experience of Christian liturgy. The best of constructive feminist theology attempts to take seriously Vatican II's insistence on the need for humble self-examination and ongoing reform in the life of the church, so that the relationships within the church—in this between men and women—might be a more faithful reflection of the divine regards for all human persons. As Hilkert observed, many feminists experience themselves as a "loyal opposition" while others are "in exile," having made a home in other Christian communities.[7]

More recently, studies that focus on the contributions and experience of women at the Second Vatican Council have begun to emerge. Carmel McEnroy has written the most extensive account to date of the women—ten religious and thirteen laywomen—who took part in the third and fourth sessions of the council in 1963 and 1964, aptly titled *Guests in Their Own House*.[8] Certainly, there is need for more critical study in order to gain a fuller picture of their contributions. A look at some of the most significant contributions of the women auditors provides some important clues for understanding the treatment of the subject of women in the council documents.

The Participation of Women at Vatican II

Remarkably, although they were invited as something of an afterthought and were never granted the right to address the council *in aula* as were several of their male counterparts, twenty-three women took part in the council as official auditors. It was the first time in history—perhaps since the convocation of the Second Council of Nicaea in 787 by the Empress Irene, acting as regent for her son, the Emperor Constantine IV— that a woman took part in an ecumenical council.[9] Women were invited to attend the third and fourth sessions of Vatican II as auditors after a number of bishops lamented their absence.[10]

A number of laymen had been present from the middle of the first session of the council as auditors. Six of them would address the bishops on different occasions, speaking to the debates on ecumenism, on the apostolate of the laity, and on the "Pastoral Constitution on the Church in the Modern World." Notably, whenever one of these lay auditors addressed the council, the texts of their interventions were prepared and agreed upon together with all the auditors, including the women. Although none of the lay auditors had an effective vote in the council, many contributed significant elements to the drafting of the conciliar documents. Some sat on conciliar subcommissions.[11] When this was not possible, they conveyed their concerns, including critiques of the draft schemata and constructive proposals for their revision, in exchanges with receptive bishops in the wings of official debate, in both public and private meetings.

Women auditors were selected for their leadership in a number of significant international organizations for religious and laywomen. Not unlike the case of the bishops, their backgrounds and perspectives on the council and its deliberations varied widely. Marie-Louise Monnet was the first laywoman to cross the threshold of St. Peter's Basilica to attend a general congregation. She had founded a number of Catholic Action groups for youth in France and was President of MIAMSI, the Mouvement International d'Apostolat des Milieux Sociaux Indépendants. Pilar Bellosillo of Spain was the leader of the World Union of Catholic Women's Organizations (WUCWO). Rosemary Goldie of Australia was Executive Secretary of the Permanent Council for the International Congress on the Lay Apostolate (COPECIAL). Following the council she was appointed to the staff of the Pontifical Council for the Laity, the first woman to hold a permanent post within the Roman curia. Luz Maria Longoria and her husband, José Alvarez Icaza Manero, co-presidents of the Christian

Family Movement, had the auspicious task of representing tens of thousands of Catholic families from around the world. To prepare for the council, they consulted members of the movement by means of an extensive survey and a thirty-six-country tour.[12]

Mary Luke Tobin, a Sister of Loretto, was the leader of the newly established Leadership Conference for Women Religious in the United States. She was joined by two other American women: Sister Claudia Feddish, Superior General of the Sisters of the Eastern congregation of St. Basil the Great, and Catherine McCarthy, president of the National Council of Catholic Women. Sister Jerome Chimy of Canada represented another Eastern Catholic religious order, the Servants of Mary Immaculate, and attended the final session of the council in the fall of 1965.

Luz and José Alvarez Icaza contributed directly to the bishops' deliberations on the ends of marriage. Their personal contributions and those of the wider Christian Family Movement weighed heavily in *Gaudium et Spes's* treatment of the ends of marriage.[13] Sexual relations were no longer portrayed as a "remedy for concupiscence." Moving beyond the juridical approach to the sacrament that had dominated in Catholic teaching, the council now presented marriage as a mutual covenant between spouses whose self-giving love is expressed in conjugal intimacy. The unitive and procreative dimensions of marriage are presented as complementary (*GS*, 48, 50).

Louise Monnet contributed significantly to the text on the apostolate of the laity read *in aula* by the Englishman Patrick Keegan, President of the International Young Catholic Workers movement.[14] Economist Barbara Ward, another woman consultant, though not an official auditor, drafted significant portions of the intervention delivered by James Norris, an Executive for Catholic Relief Services and a lay auditor, when he addressed the council on the issue of poverty. Following the council, Ward played a leading role as an advisor to the Pontifical Council for Justice and Peace. She would address the 1971 Synod of Bishops on Justice in the World. Lay auditors contributed significantly to the elaboration of the "Pastoral Constitution on the Church in the Modern World" and the "Decree on the Apostolate of the Laity." The religious women among the auditors, however, were not as warmly welcomed by the commission responsible for the drafting of the "Decree on the Adaptation and Renewal of Religious Life," *Perfectae Caritatis*, and were repeatedly rebuffed by its president, Cardinal Antoniutti. In all cases women were left without a direct voice. Yet their influence was unmistakable.

Vatican II's Teaching on Women

The council's teaching provided for several important advances and set the door ajar for more direct involvement of women in the teaching, ministry, and daily witness of the church. The "Pastoral Constitution on the Church," *Gaudium et Spes*, acknowledges the aspirations of women within the human community, affirming that today "women claim equality with men in law and in reality, where they have not yet reached it" (*GS*, 9). The constitution underlines the essential equality of women and men as the basis of social justice for all, insisting: "Since all men and women…created in the image of God have the same nature and the same origin, and since they have all been redeemed by Christ and enjoy the same divine calling and destiny, the basic equality which they all share needs to be increasingly recognized" (*GS*, 29). In the light of the equal dignity of women and men, any discrimination on the basis of sex is deemed "contrary to the purpose of God" (*GS*, 29). The council deplores the fact that women continue to be denied their basic human rights when they are the object of human trafficking (*GS*, 27), when they are "denied the choice of husband or state of life, or opportunities for education and culture equal to those of men" (*GS*, 29; cf. 60).

With regard to the participation of women in the life of the church, the "Decree on the Apostolate of the Laity," *Apostolicam Actuositatem*, declares:

"since women are increasingly taking an active part in the whole life of society, it is important that their participation in the various fields of the church's apostolate should also increase" (*AA*, 9). It is recognized that laymen and women today are more deeply aware of their dignity as sharers in the priestly, prophetic, and kingly office of Christ, and of the coresponsibility in mission that flows from it. Therefore, "Laypeople with a truly apostolic mind, after the manner of those men and women who assisted Paul in the preaching of the gospel (see Acts 18:18, 26; Rom 16:3)," work in the service of their sisters and brothers in Christ. "They cooperate energetically in passing on the word of God, especially by catechetical instruction," as well as through the "care of souls" and the "administration of the church's goods" (*AA*, 10). To carry out these tasks, the council recognizes the need for adequate formation, including access to theological education (*AA*, 32; cf. *AG*, 17). These men and women who "preside over prayers" and "teach doctrine" ought to enjoy "a decent standard of living and social security" provided through a "just wage" (*AG*, 17). *Lumen Gentium* acknowledges that although the majority of the baptized faithful will live their witness to the gospel in the ordinary activities of their daily lives—in caring for their families, in their daily employment at school, in factories, and offices— some men and women experience a call to devote themselves to a more explicitly ecclesial form of ministry in the service of the people of God "like the women and men who assisted the apostle Paul in the gospel, working hard in the Lord (Rom 16:3 ff)" (*LG*, 33).

The substance of these teachings is almost taken for granted today. At the time of the Second Vatican Council, they signified substantial progress in understanding the role of women in the life of the church and society. These few lines of teaching opened the way for women to devote themselves to new forms of pastoral ministry and to the study and teaching of theology. In the fifty years that have transpired since Vatican II, women have come to play a major role in the pastoral life of the church, so that today they represent the vast majority of lay ecclesial ministers in North America and in many other regions of the world. Women have also taken their place in the college of theologians, where they make significant contributions to the study of the scriptures and to theological reflection in the service of the church and its mission.

Interpreting the "Silence" of the Council on the Role of Women

At the outset of this chapter, we noted that the documents of Vatican II do not contain an extended reflection in the role of women as a distinct and uniquely identifiable group within the structure of the church. This apparent silence does not mean that women's voices were ignored; rather, it confirms that they had been heard. The 1963 draft of the decree on the laity contained two articles which treated men (*De Viris*) and women (*De Mulieribus*) separately. The women at the council preferred to be considered under the inclusive heading of the generic "men" (*hominum*) over being exalted in flowery discourse, or defined according to rigid categories. Pilar Bellosillo cautioned those well-intentioned bishops who, in their exuberance, were looking for ways to elaborate a poetic tribute to women. "That kind of language is detached from life and puts women on a pedestal instead of on the same level as man."[15] By using idealistic language, she argued, they actually betray an attitude that takes man to be the measure of humanity and undermines the equal dignity of women. Few women could identify with the poetic image that they were proposing. In a similar exchange, Rosemary Goldie pointed out to a commission member, "You can omit all those gratuitous flowery adjectives, the pedestals and incense, from your sentence. All women ask for is that they be recognized as the full human persons they are, and treated accordingly."[16]

The women at Vatican II understood themselves to be included fully each time the council referred to the members of the baptized faithful. During the drafting of *Gaudium et Spes*, Rosemary Goldie was invited to convey the views of the auditors on whether the council should speak concerning women. She replied in the affirmative, yet qualifying her answer: "on condition that women are not isolated as a problem apart, as it were on the fringe of society and the modern world, or as if the real problems that women experience were their exclusive concern."[17] Thanks to interventions like these by the women at Vatican II, the council's teaching refrains from adopting a theology of "complementarity" or of ascribing a set of charisms to women and another to men, one role for women and another for men. Its approach is, rather, an inclusive one. The baptized faithful are not defined according to gender roles but in accord with their participation in the mystery of Christ through baptism, a condition shared equally by all members of the church. Any attempt to carry out a feminist reading of the teachings of Vatican II must be mindful of the council's resolve to present women as self-conscious, self-determining, and full participants in the life of church and society. The council's apparent silence on the question of women should not be mistaken for the exclusion of women's perspectives.

Outside the council hall at Vatican II, more militant women were beginning to raise the question of sexism and to argue in support of women's participation in ordained ministry. Their concerns were voiced by the likes of Gertrud Heinzelmann of Switzerland, who addressed a pointed petition to the Preparatory Commission entitled *Wir schweigen nicht länger* ("We Will Not Keep Silent Any Longer").[18] Feminist scholars sought to build on the impulse of reform at work in the council. In the decades that followed Vatican II, many were frustrated by the speed at which debate on the question of women's ordination was preempted by Pope Paul VI[19] and Pope John Paul II.[20] While it had not created a space for a fulsome reflection on the question of women or of women in ministry, Vatican II did prepare the way for the gifts of women to be more widely recognized and welcomed into the life of the church. However modest its advances, the council's teaching created the conditions for a significant evolution in the roles of women in the life of the church in the postconciliar years.

The recent election of Pope Francis seems to hold some promise for the possibility of reflecting on the many developments of the past half century to consider how, in our own day, the contributions and the voices of women might be more fully integrated into the structures and decisional bodies of the church. The growing recognition of the dignity of women and the desire to see women respected as full and equal partners in the life of the church and society is one of the signs of the times named by the Second Vatican Council. This new awareness brought with it the concomitant responsibility to reverse the effects of sexism and patriarchy, as feminist scholars continue to remind us. Together with all the baptized faithful, the women at Vatican II were imbued with a profound new awareness of their calling and responsibility for proclaiming the gospel in the world. It is to this new sense of responsibility in the face of history that we now turn.

Part IV

A NEW ECCLESIAL
CONSCIOUSNESS

IDENTITY AND CONTINGENCY

In parts I and II, we see the extent to which the drama of Vatican II and debates concerning its interpretation in the postconciliar period have focused largely on the relationship of the church to the modern world. Related to this is the question of history. In a world in which church and state were increasingly recognized as distinct and autonomous realities, and where religious pluralism had become a fact of life, the question of the relationship of the church and contemporary culture was now raised in a new way. No longer relying on the coercion— however blatant or subtle—of the state or social convention, Catholic Christians were compelled to recognize that the only means at its disposal to promote the values of the gospel in the world is the authenticity of its own witness. The council clearly recognizes the "world" as an ambivalent reality marked at once by human sin and the promise of gospel values. This is especially true of *Gaudium et Spes's* descriptions of the crises facing the world in mid-twentieth century (*GS*, 4).

The council's teaching reveals a sense of ecclesial identity that no longer conceives of the church as a "perfect society," in the preferred language of controversialist theology, but views it according to the biblical paradigm of a pilgrim people of God *in* the world, moving through history. Gérard Philips explained in his redactional history of *Lumen Gentium* that chapter 2 on the people of God follows on chapter 1, which treats the mystery of the church, "to show how the mystery of the church is accomplished in history."[1] Vatican II's ecclesiology is thus marked by a new historical mindedness. The church speaks here with a sense of its own historicity. The people of God stands in constant need of purification and reform (*LG*, 6; *UR*, 4, 6) until it reaches its final eschatological fulfilment. This humbler sense of self-identity is linked to a growing awareness of the church's need to be in dialogue with others, a dialogue characterized as a mutual exchange in which she is both witness and apprentice.

A New Stage of Human History

When Pope Benedict XVI spoke of the necessity of a "hermeneutic of reform" that involves a complex matrix of both continuity and change for a correct interpretation of the Second Vatican Council, he noted the important role played by the programmatic speeches of Pope John XXIII and Pope Paul VI in defining the council's reforming task. One of the most striking features of those speeches is the frequent reference to the importance of history. In the dialectic between the events of world history and the historical consciousness of the church, we witness the emergence of a renewed and self-reflexive sense of responsibility in the Catholic community of believers. Equally present is the awareness of what Pope Benedict has referred to as the contingency and limitations in the form of church teaching and practice.

Let us recall for a moment the historical context of the conciliar event. Pope John XXIII called for the Second Vatican Council in the wake of the Second World War. Many saw the destruction inflicted by the two world wars and the annihilation of six million Jews as a profound failure on the part of a "Christian" civilization. In Africa and Asia, developing nations were seeking independence from colonial powers. The age of manned space flight had begun. It was the height of the Cold War between the North Atlantic Alliance and the Soviet Union. The opening ceremonies of the council were broadcast around the world on radio and television by means of new satellite technology. Less than a week after the council began, President John F. Kennedy ordered a military blockade in response to the deployment of Soviet nuclear missiles on the island of Cuba threatening to annihilate the most important population centers on the North American continent. The times were marked by a profound awareness of humanity's capacity for self-destruction, and yet of its immense creative capacity and progress.

In the letter of convoking the council issued on Christmas day of 1961, John XXIII wrote, "Today the church is witnessing a crisis underway within society. While humanity is on the edge of a new era, tasks of immense gravity and amplitude await the church, as in the most tragic periods of its history. It is a question in fact of bringing the modern world into contact with the vivifying and perennial energies of the Gospel."[2] While noting the challenge of materialism and rising atheism, Pope John sought to awaken in the church what he called "the sense of responsibility." Rather than see only darkness, he called on the members of the church to discern the presence and activity of God's Spirit in this moment of history: "We…like to affirm all our confidence in Our Saviour, Who has not left the world which he redeemed. Indeed, we make ours the recommendation of Jesus that one should know how to distinguish the 'signs of the times' (Matt 16:3), and we seem to see now, in the midst of so much darkness, a few indications which may augur well for the fate of the Church and for humanity."[3]

The Gospel of Matthew recounts how Jesus exhorted the Pharisees and Sadducees, who were asking for an extraordinary sign from God, to be attentive to what God was already accomplishing before their eyes (Matt 16:1–4). Reading the "signs of the times" requires a readiness to recognize, in every age of human history, those places where the grace of God has prepared the way or laid a foundation upon which we might build a better world. Among these signs, Pope John named the growing recognition of the dignity of the human person, the desire for peace among the nations, and for Christian unity. The church, he noted, did not remain a "lifeless spectator" before new movements of social change and technological progress. While the world had changed, the Christian community as well was "in great part transformed and renewed," and "more conscious of its responsibilities."[4] Remarkably, Pope John testified to a change and renewal in the collective consciousness of the church even before the council had begun to outline its program for an updating or reform of ecclesial life—indeed, before a single bishop had arrived in Rome to begin the actual deliberations of the council! The council, then, emerged as a response to a particular moment in history, one that impinged on the church's own sense of mission and identity. The reforms undertaken at Vatican II are an expression of this renewed self-reflexive ecclesial consciousness.

In his opening speech to the council fathers, delivered on October 11, 1962, Pope John XXIII begged to differ with the "prophets of doom" around him who saw nothing but "prevarication and ruin" in the modern world. He complained that "they had learned nothing from history, which is, nonetheless, the great teacher of life." He saw the world differently. "In the present order of things," he declared, "Divine Providence is leading us to a new order of human relations which, by men's efforts and even beyond their very expectations, are directed toward the fulfilment of God's superior and inscrutable designs. And everything, even human differences, leads to the greater good of the church."[5] People were coming together in ways never seen before to work for peace, justice, and harmony. Pope John observed a strengthening in the collective consciousness of humanity, a new ordering of human relationships in the global community that now required a shift in the church's self-understanding and in its relationship with others.

Pope John's confidence in the Lord of history was quickly transposed into a desire on the part of the council fathers to express the solidarity and compassion of the church with all of humanity. Already on October 20, 1962, less than ten days after the official opening of the first session and in the midst of the Cuban missile crisis, the bishops endorsed and published a "Message to the World." Declaring their commitment to "renew themselves," they presented an image of a church that was "not to dominate but to serve" all of humanity (Matt 20:28; 1 John 3:16). They wrote, "United here from every nation under heaven, we carry in our hearts the anxieties of all peoples entrusted to us, the anxieties of body and soul, sorrows and desires, and hopes. We turn our mind constantly toward all the anxieties afflicting men [sic] today. Our concern is directed especially to the more humble, the more poor."[6]

The words of the council's "Message to the World" are a foreshadowing of the council's "Pastoral Constitution on the Church in the Modern World," *Gaudium et Spes*, the only document that can be said to be a "child of the council," in the sense that it was not anticipated in any of the preparatory texts. The opening lines of *Gaudium et Spes* are among the most frequently cited of all the council documents, as they express perhaps more than any other the momentous turn to the world that distinguished Vatican II from previous ecumenical councils: "The joys and hopes, the sorrows and anxieties of people today, especially of those who are poor and afflicted, are also the joys and hopes, sorrows and anxieties of the disciples of Christ, and there is nothing truly human which does not also affect them" (*GS*, 1).

The original inspiration for the "Message to the World" came from the French Dominican Marie-Dominique Chenu.[7] Chenu was among those European theologians who, in the period between the two wars, became deeply preoccupied by the failure of the church to communicate the gospel in a meaningful way to contemporary people, in particular to the working classes. Battered by the shock of the Enlightenment, the French Revolution, and a series of confrontations with the rising nation states of Europe that systematically and at times violently unseated the church from long-held centers of temporal power, Catholicism took on "a new sociological form" that differed from the form of earlier times. Joseph Komonchak contended that in the nineteenth and early twentieth centuries "modern Roman Catholicism took the form of a counter-society, legitimated by a counter-culture, as a response, and in opposition to the emerging liberal society which advanced with such inexorability."[8] An anti-Enlightenment, anti-Protestant, and antimodern stance characterized the official self-definition of Catholicism and was conveyed in the teaching of the popes from this same period. Catholicism evolved its own cultural ethos in a virtually closed, parallel society, isolated from the world. Among the effects of this "ghetto mentality" was an unintended "divorce of faith from life" and a privatization of religious practice.[9]

It was this gap between the church and contemporary society, this failure to engage, that moved a theologian like Chenu to reflect upon the mission and identity of the church in the world. In "creating for the church a world apart from the world,"[10] the Christian faith had been stripped of its most basic context—the history into which the Word of God had entered through the Incarnation. Chenu insisted that a renewed self-understanding of the church, including a renewed presence of the church in the world, would be required if the Christian community was to live out its mission with any effect. He recognized that technological progress and the structuring of modern societies had profoundly changed the nature of humanity's relationship to the created world. Human communities experienced a new capacity and responsibility for shaping the world. This brought with it a new collective consciousness and a sense of participation in a common enterprise, creating a dynamic of solidarity. In this new context, the age of a new Christianity, a strategy of witness would supplant that of conquest, which had dominated in the age of Christendom.[11] A dialogical discourse would replace the language of condemnation and condescension. The council itself would recover an understanding of the centrality and the consequences of the Incarnation of Christ for human history, a notion deeply embedded in the theology of the early church fathers (GS, 32; AG, 3).

The council's "Pastoral Constitution on the Church in the Modern World" observes that the global community "finds itself today in a new stage of human history" marked by rapid and profound change. This social and cultural transformation is not without effect on "the life of religion" (*GS*, 4). *Gaudium et Spes* links the profound changes of modern social and cultural life in this "new age" (*GS*, 54) to a renewed sense of responsibility in the collective conscience of the human community:

> There is a growing number of men and women in every country who are conscious of being architects and authors of the culture of their own community. Throughout the world there is a continual increase in the awareness of autonomy as well as of responsibility, which is of greatest significance for the spiritual and moral maturity of humankind. This is more evident if we consider the unification of the world in terms of truth and justice. Thus we are witnesses that a new humanism is being born in which the human is defined above all in terms of our responsibility to our sisters and brothers and to history. (*GS*, 55)

The members of the church share in this heightened sense of responsibility or of coresponsibility with others for giving shape to a more just world that is characteristic of this new age of humanity. When combined with an awareness of the dignity of all persons created in the image of God, this "sense of responsibility" can be placed at the service of the common good (*GS*, 31).

A renewed ecclesial consciousness leads as well to a new sense of responsibility for the self-realization of the church in its social and historical form, including the form of its doctrinal self-expression. During the council's third session, when the lay auditor Patrick Keegan addressed the council fathers concerning the proposed "Decree on the Apostolate of the Laity," he observed: "The schema is a natural outcome of the church's new awareness of herself. It is also the result of the progressive discovery by men and women of their responsibility and role within the whole apostolate of the church."[12] Pope John XXIII had linked the evolving sense of the church's identity and mission to the pastoral purpose of the council and the form that the bishops would give to their doctrinal teaching. As we saw in part II, the pastoral and doctrinal dimensions of the council's teaching were closely bound from the outset.

The Pastoral Character of the Council

It was in light of the changing context of human history that Pope John XXIII called the council to find a way or a "method of presenting the truth" that would be more in conformity with "a magisterium which is predominantly pastoral in character."[13] In one of the final exchanges with his personal secretary, Loris Cappovilla, he confided, "the circumstances of our day, the growing needs of the last fifty years, and a deeper doctrinal understanding have led us to a new reality, as I said in my opening speech to the council. It is not the gospel that is changing. It is that we have begun to better understand it."[14] In reminding the council fathers of the important distinction between the "substance" of the faith and the "way in which it is presented," John XXIII underlined the historicity of the tradition, in particular the contingent nature of its doctrinal expression and social form. Further, by insisting that the "salient point" of the council must be this attention to the pastoral character of church teaching, he was inviting the bishops to allow the consideration of the receivers of their teaching to shape the form of the council's doctrinal expression.

Pope Paul VI would recall this principle in his speech to the council fathers at the opening of the second session. The "pastoral aim" of the council was "to consider how to expound church teaching in a manner demanded by the times."[15] Referring to his predecessor, he observed:

You have awakened in the conscience of the teaching authority of the church the conviction that Christian doctrine is not merely truth to be investigated by reason illumined by faith, but teaching that can generate life and action; and that the authority of the church is not limited to condemning contrary errors, but extends to the communication of positive and vital doctrine, the source of its fecundity.[16]

A Renewed Understanding of the Pastoral Teaching Office

Pope John XXIII had called attention to a fuller understanding of the exercise of the pastoral teaching office of the bishops. In his subtle differentiation between the content and form of church doctrine, he invited them to better appreciate the distinction between tradition as that which has been received through the gift of God's self-revelation, and tradition as the act of transmission or process of handing it on. At Vatican II we see a shift from a magisterium centered primarily on the content of faith to one that gave an unprecedented attention to form. The former understood its role as one of repeating an accumulation of propositional "truth statements," where revealed truth was virtually identified with unchanging doctrinal formula. The latter is a magisterium that understands its primary responsibility as one of communication, the transmission of a message. It is founded on a personalist and trinitarian theology of revelation, such as we find in the "Dogmatic Constitution on Divine Revelation" (*DV*, 2–6)—a message rooted in the experience of personal encounter with Christ that, when received, has the power to transform persons and communities and ground a new set of relationships in communion.

Attention to the pastoral character or form of church teaching does not imply diminished concern for the content of faith. Nevertheless, by attending to the receivers of their teaching, the bishops were led to a deeper understanding of the exercise of their pastoral teaching office, which is at the service of the church's fidelity to the gospel. Maintaining the tradition of the apostles is an important aspect of this office and is an inherently conservative task. However, the exercise of the pastoral teaching office also involves the responsibility to nourish the living faith of the church in the present, to make the message of the gospel "actual" in the here and now. The bishops must attend to the memory of the teaching of the apostles, yet exercise their creative responsibility to realize the expression of that living faith in each moment of history, in each culture and local church. Their task is at once doctrinal and pastoral—to teach the faith and attend to its reception.

The Second Vatican Council is an ecumenical council whose teaching reflects a unique concern for the creative responsibility of the pastoral teaching office where the bishops adopted a style of doctrinal teaching aimed at engaging in dialogue with contemporaries, believers and nonbelievers alike.

This style of doctrinal expression, without parallel in previous ecumenical councils, in no way diminishes the doctrinal authority of Vatican II's teaching. Pondering the interdependence of the pastoral and doctrinal nature of the council's teachings, Marie-Dominique Chenu writes,

> This entire council is pastoral, in the sense that the church is becoming aware of its mission. This entire council is doctrinal, because its aim is to make the presence of the gospel real through and in the church. How sensationally original! A council which, without ignoring the errors, the misdeeds, and the darknesses of the present time, is not tensed up and hostile to them, but recognizes in this age's hopes and values so many implicit appeals to the gospel; in them it finds the material for and a legitimation of a dialogue.[17]

Paul VI reflected upon Vatican II's dialogical style when he addressed the last general session of the council on December 7, 1965:

> The teaching authority of the church, even though not wishing to issue extraordinary doctrinal pronouncements, has made thoroughly known its authoritative teaching on a number of questions which today weigh upon man's [sic] conscience and activity, descending, so to speak, into a dialogue with him, but ever preserving its own authority and force; it has spoken with the

accommodating friendly voice of pastoral charity; its desire has been to be heard and understood by everyone; it has not merely concentrated on intellectual understanding but has also sought to express itself in simple, up-to-date, conversational style, derived from actual experience and a cordial approach which make it more vital, attractive and persuasive; it has spoken to modern man [sic] as he is.[18]

He observes, further, that the council's teaching is directed to enabling the church to live its vocation in the service of humankind. Its pastoral character is a consequence of the necessity for the church to engage in dialogue with all peoples and with contemporary human values. The dialogical character of the council's teaching is another important key to a proper interpretation of the council, as we see in part V.

Part V

IDENTITY, DIALOGUE, AND REFORM

Dialogue is a recurrent theme in the teaching of Vatican II. John O'Malley has helped us to appreciate how the unique rhetorical style that distinguishes the documents of Vatican II from the doctrinal teaching of previous ecumenical councils is modelled on the discourse of the Greco-Roman classics and on the style of early Christian writings. Its panegyric discourse paints an idealized portrait in an effort to inspire and incite emulation, to reach the human heart and inspire it to action. This new style is reflected in the acquisition of a new vocabulary, with the use of many "horizontal words" like "brother and sister" or "people of God," and "reciprocity words" such as "cooperation," "partnership," and "collaboration." He noted as well the frequent use of "humility words" such as "pilgrim people" and "servant." O'Malley observed, "there is scarcely a page in the council documents on which [the word] 'dialogue' or its equivalent does not occur."[1] With a heightened historical consciousness, the council sought to renew both the expression of Catholic self-identity and the Catholic Church's relationships with others. A defining feature of this renewed identity and missional engagement can be seen in the adoption of a fundamentally dialogical attitude toward others.

Pope Paul VI provided a rich reflection on the need for this outward turn and for the adoption of a fundamental disposition of dialogue in his much neglected encyclical letter "On the Church," *Ecclesiam Suam*, published on August 6, 1964, midway through the council.[2] This letter can be seen as giving expression not only to his personal views, but also to the consensus emerging from the bishops assembled at the council concerning the task facing the church.[3] In the period leading up to the council, a number of influential bishops had expressed their misgivings concerning the draft documents submitted to the bishops by the Preparatory Commission. Many were written in the scholastic language and juridical style of the past. If the goal of the council was to speak to contemporary men and women and to help the church be more engaged with the modern world, they feared it could fail miserably without a substantial change in approach. Cardinal Léger of Montreal wrote an impassioned plea to Pope John XXIII, co-signed by six other leading cardinals, to convey his concern.[4] They proposed that the council adopt a more positive and pastoral approach.[5]

Their efforts helped to shape the discourse of Pope John in the speeches he delivered on the eve of the council and at the opening session.

Pope Paul VI carried forward these priorities that Pope John had identified with the "pastoral aim" of the council, and now gave it a practical form. He called for a commitment to ongoing dialogue within the church and extending in a series of concentric circles to include other Christians, other religions, nonbelievers, and the modern world. He modelled that dialogical engagement throughout the conciliar period when he undertook three emblematic voyages: to the Holy Land in January of 1964, where he met with the Ecumenical Patriarch Athenagoras of Constantinople[6] and with Jewish leaders; to India, "the cradle of great religions,"[7] in December of 1964, where he wept with the poor and the sick; and finally, to New York, where, in October of 1965, he addressed a special assembly of the United Nations expressing the commitment of the Catholic Church to work with all peoples for the promotion of justice and peace.[8] These were the first travels of any pope outside of Italy since the nineteenth century.

Dialogue is found at the heart of a threefold program proposed by Pope Paul's encyclical to orient the council and the subsequent activity of the church in service to the human community. The first element of his program is a deeper self-understanding of the nature and mission of the church. A heightened consciousness of ecclesial identity, he argued, must be accompanied by a realistic assessment of the distance between the "ideal image" of the church intended by Christ and the "actual image" presented by the contemporary community of believers.[9] The church's consciousness is reflexive and self-critical, at once aware of its high calling as community of grace and of its limits and failings as a community of repentant sinners. Honest and humble self-examination leads to the second element of Pope Paul's program, namely, a commitment to undertake whatever reforms are deemed necessary for the renewal of the life and witness of the church, in order that it might reflect that ideal image more faithfully.[10] The task of *metanoia* or conversion was not only to guide the council's work of updating the church; it was to be a permanent feature of ecclesial life as the church continues to grow in its understanding of the gospel and in fidelity to its message.[11] Finally, this self-reflexive activity and the missional engagement of the church are to be sustained by "friendly dialogue."[12]

Pope Paul underlined that "the noble origin of this dialogue [is] in the mind of God."[13] The motive for the church's engagement in dialogue is more than a desire to practice effective methods of communication. Pope Paul and the Second Vatican Council envision the whole history of salvation and of God's revelation as a conversation initiated by God, who has spoken an incomparable and self-revealing Word of love for all humanity in the incarnation, death, and resurrection of Christ. The "model and source" of dialogue and communion to which the church is called is to be found in the mutual exchange of life among the three divine persons of the Trinity (*UR*, 2). Thus, the exchange of dialogue is a reflection of the inner nature of the church, which exists to serve as an instrument of God's "dialogue of salvation" with all humanity.[14]

Dialogue in the Council's Teaching

Vatican II's "Declaration on Religious Freedom," *Dignitatis Humanae*, provides a clue to understanding the role of dialogue in the pursuit of truth. While it affirms the right of every person to follow the dictates of their conscience, it also recognizes the responsibility of all to seek the truth. This truth seeking is not something we can do alone. It is a shared undertaking. "Truth, however, is to be sought in a manner befitting the dignity and social nature of the human person, namely by free enquiry assisted by teaching and instruction, and by exchange and dialogue in which people explain to each other the truth as they have discovered it or as they see it, so as to assist each other in their search" (*DH*, 3). Authentic dialogue is neither a strategy susceptible to relativism, nor a ploy to impose one's point of view. Fundamentally, it is a common search for truth.

Pope Paul's three-point program is more fully developed in the "Decree on Ecumenism" than in any other conciliar document. Here it is affirmed that whenever Catholics enter into dialogue with other Christians, they are led not only to "acknowledge and esteem the truly Christian endowments" present in other churches. In surprising ways, the experience of dialogue leads participants to be more deeply aware of their particular ecclesial identities, including the strengths and limitations of their concrete expression of faith. Catholics in dialogue with other Christians are to be mindful of "their especial duty...to make a careful and honest appraisal of whatever needs to be renewed in the catholic household itself" so that its life and teaching are a more faithful reflection of the gospel (*UR*, 4). The "Decree on Ecumenism" links the experience of dialogue to the "continual reformation" of which the church has need in order to overcome "deficiencies" in moral life and church discipline, and even in "the way that church teaching has been formulated" (*UR*, 6). The reform of moral conduct, church discipline, and practice, and of the expression of doctrine itself, is deemed necessary whenever these become an obstacle to the effective witness to the gospel. The "Decree on Ecumenism" echoes *Lumen Gentium*'s ecclesiology of the church as the messianic people of God, a pilgrim people firmly rooted in all the contingencies of human history, a community that is "at one and the same time holy and always in need of purification" and renewal (*LG*, 8).

The council acknowledges that the dialogical relationship between the church and the world is not unidirectional. It is a dialectical exchange in which each influences the other. As a human community, and one that is called to be a sacrament and sign for all of humanity (*LG*, 1), the pilgrim people of God is a learning community and receives much from all that is truly human in its pursuit of the truth. In its reflection on the task of the church in today's world, *Gaudium et Spes* does not hesitate to affirm that while the church has much to offer to modern society (*GS*, 42), "the church is equally conscious of how much it needs to learn" from its relationship with the world (*GS*, 43). Its teaching offers a vital clue to understanding how the Second Vatican Council understood what it was doing, in effect, as it undertook the task of updating and reform.

Just as it is important for the world to recognize the church as a social reality and agent in history, so the church is also aware of how much it has received from the history and development of the human race. The experience of past centuries, the advances in the sciences, and the treasures hidden in the various forms of human culture, which disclose human nature more completely and indicate new ways to the truth, are of benefit also to the church. From the beginning of its history, it has learned to express Christ's message in the concepts and languages of various peoples, and it has tried to throw light on it through the wisdom of philosophers, aiming so far as proper to suit the gospel to the grasp of everyone as well as the expectations of the wise. This adaptation in preaching the revealed word should remain the law of all evangelization (*GS*, 44).

This frank admission of the church's reliance upon the developments of science, culture, and philosophy in coming to understand and express the message of the gospel "in better terms" (*GS*, 44) reflects a profound awareness of the contingency and historicity of Christian doctrine. The "law of all evangelization" is that in every age, and in every new context, the church must be actively engaged in the act of "listen[ing] to the various voices of our day," weighing and discerning them in the light of God's Word (*GS*, 44). It is through this constant exchange and dialogue with the contemporary world that the church will continue to grow in understanding, appropriating, and better expressing the gift of God's revelation.

The continual process of dialogue and discernment, of receiving insights from the experience of contemporary science and culture and weighing them in light of God's Word, is not a task reserved to an elite group within the church. As we saw in part II, the mystery of God's self-revelation in Christ is entrusted to all the baptized faithful. God's Spirit continues to guide and enlighten their common sense of faith. Together the laity, religious, theologians, and bishops continue to probe the scriptures and read the signs of the times. Together they grow in understanding the tradition of faith that has been handed on to us, "both the words and the realities they signify." They come to a deeper penetration of faith "through contemplation and study," through the experience of the spiritual life, and through the preaching of the bishops in the exercise of their authoritative teaching office. The council's "Dogmatic Constitution on Divine Revelation" affirms by these few lines the principle of doctrinal development, recognizing that the truth is not a possession of the church. Rather, the church is born by the truth on its pilgrim way, on a journey "towards the fullness of God's truth" (*DV*, 8). Our understanding of the mystery of God will not be exhausted until the church reaches her eschatological fulfilment in the end times. While we await that fulfilment, God's "dialogue of salvation" with humanity takes place in and through the community established by his Word. For this reason, dialogue among all the baptized faithful is a crucial resource for discerning the *sensus fidelium*, the Spirit-led judgment of the whole church.

Perhaps the strongest exhortation to dialogue within the church is found in the council's "Pastoral Constitution on the Church in the Modern World," which links the practice of dialogue among all the baptized faithful to the heart of the church's calling.

> In virtue of its mission to spread the light of the gospel's message over the entire globe, and to bring all people of whatever nation, race or culture together into the one Spirit, the church comes to be a sign of that kinship which makes genuine dialogue possible and vigorous. This requires us first of all to promote mutual esteem, respect and harmony, with the recognition of all legitimate diversity, in the church itself, in order to establish ever more fruitful exchanges among all who make up the one people of God, both pastors and the rest of the faithful. For what unites the faithful is stronger than what divides them: there should be unity in essentials, freedom in doubtful matters, and charity in everything. (*GS*, 92)

The real significance of this text becomes more apparent when it is read against the background of *Lumen Gentium*'s insistence that the church is called to be a sign and a sacrament of the unity and communion that God intends for all of humanity (*LG*, 1). It suggests that if the church wishes to promote dialogue and unity among the nations, its own inner life must be a model of that dynamic exchange which nourishes communion.

As part of its program for ecclesial reform, the Second Vatican Council sought to renew traditional synodal structures and encouraged the development of new ones in order to facilitate dialogue within the church. Among those described in the "Decree on the Pastoral Office of Bishops," *Christus Dominus*, are the international synod of bishops (*CD*, 5),[15] regional conferences of bishops (*CD*, 35:5; 38:1–5), and the patriarchal synods of the Eastern Catholic Churches (*CD*, 5; 38:6) intended to promote a more collegial exercise of episcopal authority. The council calls for the renewal of the ancient practice of holding more frequent particular councils in each ecclesiastical province or within the territory of each conference of bishops (*CD*, 36). At the diocesan level, the council supports the traditional practice of holding regular diocesan synods (*CD*, 36) and encourages the establishment of pastoral councils whenever possible (*CD*, 27; *AG*, 30)[16] so that qualified representatives of the local church—ordained, religious, and laity—might work collaboratively with the bishop to determine the pastoral needs and priorities of the diocese. The ecclesiology underpinning these initiatives extends to the level of the parish where the parish pastoral council provides a forum for shared reflection and collaboration in parish pastoral planning. All of these structures are intended to be spaces of honest dialogue where together we might continue to discern the demands of gospel living and the shape of the church's mission in the service of the human family.

Dialogue and Reform Today: Crisis and Opportunity

Learning new habits of dialogue in the church demands the undoing of a deeply ingrained authoritarian culture on the one hand and of a culture of passivity on the other. The experience of the last five decades has shown that the Catholic Church has been far more effective in its institutionalized commitment to dialogue with other Christians, with Jews, and with other non-Christian religions[17] than it has been in creating spaces for genuine dialogue within its own household. Where these structures have been implemented, they have often been put into effect in a minimalist or half-hearted manner. The international synod of bishops has remained largely an instrument of the papacy and has failed to evolve into a truly collegial structure. The role of the bishops' conferences has been downgraded and almost eclipsed by an activist Roman curia. Priests complain of a lack of dialogue with their bishops. And few lay Catholics experience themselves as participating in any serious conversation that is of consequence for the life of their parish or diocesan community.

To compound the magnitude of what can only be understood as a crisis of dialogue, the Catholic community is now more than double the size that it was when the Second Vatican Council closed in 1965. Where fifty years ago the majority of Catholics lived in Europe, today two thirds of Catholics live in the southern hemisphere.[18] Never in history have we witnessed such rapid and far-reaching demographic change. We may rightly ask whether the structures of dialogue and communion envisioned by Vatican II have kept pace or are truly suited to the complex realities of the global Catholic community in the twenty-first century.

The bishops at Vatican II seized the significance of dialogue for the ongoing renewal and reform of the church. The purpose of their project of reform was not simply the modernization of the church, but the effective realization of its mission in the service of humanity. Psychology and the human sciences have helped us to understand that personal and collective identity is a dynamic reality. Identities are formed through a dialogical interaction with others. When that interaction ceases, identity becomes atrophied and disordered. Extending this analogy to the church, when structures of dialogue fail to function adequately, ecclesial self-identity is impaired and the ability of the faith community to carry out the necessary discernment and self-examination required for the ongoing renewal and reform of the church is jeopardized. A crisis of dialogue leads inexorably to a crisis of reform and to a confusion of identities.

The polarizing debate surrounding the interpretation of Vatican II that we explored in part I has distracted our attention from this very real crisis and blinded us to the opportunities facing the church in our time. Its effect has been to turn our focus inward when, as Pope Francis now reminds us, the church is called to be focused outward in mission, tending toward an encounter with God and with others.[19] The election of Pope Francis is a portent of new reforms. No sooner had Pope Benedict left the stage than we heard calls for reform from around the global Catholic community. In their pre-conclave meetings, the College of Cardinals issued an urgent plea for the next successor of Peter to undertake a serious reform of the Roman curia and of the church's governing structures in order to ensure a more collegial governance, one that respects the diversity and the subsidiarity of the local churches. Since his election, Pope Francis has spoken openly and in unvarnished terms of the need to uproot the culture of clericalism, to go out to the poor and the dispossessed, of the need for a greater recognition and integration of women's gifts, and for a pastoral solution to the present policies that exclude millions of divorced and remarried Catholics from sharing more fully in the sacramental life of the church. If his humble style of leadership is matched by substantive structural change, then his pontificate represents a significant opportunity for Catholics to embrace more fully the habits of dialogue that the Second Vatican Council sought to instill.

The election of a Latin American pope signals the coming of age of the world church that Karl Rahner witnessed coming to birth in the event of the Second Vatican Council. His move to establish an intercontinental "group of eight" cardinals and to undertake a wide-ranging consultation of the worldwide episcopate reflects a more collegial exercise of authority—one that will inevitably be more attuned to the sense of faith in the global Catholic community. Some observers have been cautious in their prognostications for Francis's pontificate, arguing that he has brought a change in style, but that we should not expect any change of church teaching or practice. Yet if Pope Francis continues to be as responsive as he has been thus far to the real challenges of setting the church on its outward, missional course, and if he succeeds in renewing the structures of ecclesial governance, he will effectively create the necessary conditions for that authentic dialogue and discernment that accompany ongoing renewal and reform.

There has not been a particularly warm welcome for Pope Francis among many traditionalist

Catholics. They complain that he is too pastoral, not sufficiently interested in doctrinal and rubrical rigor. He is too much of a free spirit, doing too many extraordinary things and not sufficiently attached to the letter of Vatican II's teaching. Bishop Bernard Fellay, heir of Archbishop Marcel Lefebvre and the present leader of the Society of Saint Pius X, has described Pope Francis as "true Modernist," the Anti-Christ predicted in the secrets of Fatima who is now leading the church into disaster.[20] These assessments echo many of the false readings of the Second Vatican Council against which the extraordinary Synod of 1985 and Pope Benedict XVI have cautioned. They continue to misconstrue the nature of tradition, mistaking it for a freeze frame of a moment in the historical past, privileging the social form of the church and its prayer in the sixteenth or nineteenth centuries. The council itself, both as a historical event and in the teaching it has placed before the church, belies the traditionalist narrative.

Pope Francis is the first pope elected since Vatican II who did not take part in the event of the council. He entered the Society of Jesus in 1958 and completed his theological education during the 1970s and 1980s, in the wake of the council. One might say that he is a "son of the council"—formed by and deeply imbued with its teaching. He is the embodiment of its message and ethos. Unlike his predecessors, he is not concerned to re-fight the battles of the council. They belong to the past. The polemicizing debate surrounding the interpretation of Vatican II has threatened to drag the church backward and turn its focus inward. Pope Francis is remarkably rooted in the present. His focus on the mission of the church to the poor has caught the imagination of many who had begun to despair that the church could once again offer a sign of hope to the world. Pope Francis represents an opportunity for a renewed reception of Vatican II, one that could potentially "release the council's bold ecclesial vision and deep-seated gospel values from decades of captivity."[21]

The Second Vatican Council was a watershed moment in history in which the Catholic Church attempted to renew itself in response to dramatic and accelerated social and cultural change, a new era of human history (*GS*, 4). In the council's teaching, the church reveals itself as deeply conscious of its agency as a responsible actor in history. This responsibility is expressed at once in the church's reflection on ecclesial identity, in its attending to the task of an ongoing self-constitution and reform, and in its engagement in service to the world. Pope Benedict XVI contends that a proper interpretation of both the event and the teaching of Vatican II requires an appreciation of how developments in history necessitated a reconsideration of the relationship between the church and the modern world, and that such an interpretation must be based upon a "hermeneutic of reform." The pastoral character of the council's teaching, together with the council's commitment to dialogue and ongoing renewal, provide an insight into the kind of reform the council sought to promote.

The documents of Vatican II are the product of a church that is acutely aware of living in a dialectical tension between the Word revealed once and for all in Christ, to which the Scriptures and Tradition of the church give witness, and the "new ways of truth"—the insights drawn from the experience of contemporary society and culture. The council itself is a hermeneutical moment—a concerted effort to reinterpret faithfully the tradition with a new historical mindedness and eschatological humility. The Jesuit theologian Christoph Theobald has suggested that Vatican II calls not only for a hermeneutic of reform, but also for a reform of hermeneutics. He rightly suggested that the council itself introduce a "new hermeneutical consciousness"[22] into the life and teaching of the church in its recognition that doctrinal teaching must be conditioned by both its pastoral purpose and historicity. Any responsible effort to interpret the teachings of the Second Vatican Council must take these dimensions into account, not only as we look back to an event that took place fifty years ago, but also as we allow its teaching to inform the life and mission of the church in our day.

NOTES

ACKNOWLEGMENTS

1. Mary Ann Hinsdale, *Women Shaping Theology* (New York: Paulist, 2006).

2. Her doctoral thesis is still required reading for anyone wishing to understand the debates at Vatican I and their implications for the reception of its teaching, including the context of Vatican II: Margaret O'Gara, *Triumph in Defeat: Infallibility, Vatican I and the French Minority Bishops* (Washington DC: Catholic University of America Press, 1988).

INTRODUCTION

1. "John's New Pentecost," *Time* (January 4, 1962), http://www.time.com/time/magazine/article/0, 9171,829723,00.html.

2. Commenting on John XXIII's calls for *aggiornamento*, Giuseppe Alberigo insists, "The Council was thus placed in the perspective of a Christian reply to the calls for the renewal of humanity." See "Transition to a New Age," in *History of Vatican II*, 5 vols., Giuseppe Alberigo and Joseph A. Komonchak, eds. (Leuven: Peeters, 1995–2006), V: 573–652, at 578.

3. "The order of bishops, which succeeds the col-

lege of apostles in teaching authority and pastoral government, and indeed in which the apostolic body continues to exist without interruption, is also subject of the supreme and full power over the universal church, provided it remains united with its head, the Roman Pontiff....The supreme power over the whole church which the college enjoys is solemnly exercised in an ecumenical council" (*LG*, 22).

4. John W. O'Malley, *What Happened at Vatican II* (Cambridge, MA: Belknap, 2008), 47–50.

5. Joseph A. Komonchak, "Interpreting the Council and its Consequences: Concluding Reflections," in James L. Heft, ed., *After Vatican II: Trajectories and Hermeneutics* (Grand Rapids, MI: Wm. B. Eerdmans, 2012), 164–72, at 164–65.

6. Joseph A. Komonchak, "The Significance of Vatican II for Ecclesiology," in Peter Phan, ed., *The Gift of the Church: A Textbook on Ecclesiology* (Collegeville, MN: Liturgical Press, 2000), 69–92, at 70.

7. Yves Congar, "Romanicité et catholicité: histoire de la conjonction changeante de deux dimensions de l'Église," *Revue de Sciences philosophiques et historiques* 71 (1987): 161–90.

8. Bernard Lonergan criticizes the decline of Catholic theology into a classicist conception of culture, which takes only one culture to be normative. Such a worldview, he declares, represents little more than a "shabby shell of catholicism." *Method in Theology* (Toronto: University of Toronto Press, 1971), 327.

9. See *UR* 4 and 6. On the role of dialogue in the council's teaching and in ecclesial life, see Catherine E. Clifford, "Learning from the Council: The Church in

112

Dialogue," *Theoforum* 44 (2013): 23–42. See also: Ann Michele Nolan, *A Privileged Moment: Dialogue in the Language of the Second Vatican Council 1962–1965* (Bern: Peter Lang, 2006).

PART I: THE HERMENEUTICS OF THE COUNCIL

1. For example, Martin Heidegger, *Being and Truth* (Bloomington, IN: Indiana UP, 2010); Hans-Georg Gadamer, *Truth and Method*. 2nd rev. ed. (New York: Continuum, 1975); and the work of Paul Ricoeur, including, by way of example, *History and Truth* (Evanston, IL: Northwestern UP, 1965); *Interpretation Theory: Discourse and the Surplus of Meaning* (Fort Worth, TX: Texas Christian UP, 1976); *Time and Narrative* (Chicago: University of Chicago Press, 1984); *From Text to Action* (Evanston, IL: Northwestern UP, 1991).

2. See Gilles Routhier, "Vatican II: Relevance and Future," *Theological Studies* 74 (2013): 537–54.

3. Gilles Routhier, "Le concile Vatican II livré aux interprétations de générations successives," *Science et Esprit* 61 (2009): 237–55, at 243. See H. R. Jauss, *Pour une esthétique de la réception* (Paris: Gallimard, 1978).

4. Massimo Faggioli, "Vatican II: The History and the Narratives," *Theological Studies* 73 (2012): 749–67.

5. A group of ten, and later twelve, cardinals appointed by the Pope to coordinate the conciliar proceedings. See Giuseppe Alberigo, *Brief History of Vatican II* (Maryknoll, NY: Orbis Books, 2006), 16–18.

6. Noted by Joseph Ratzinger in *Theological Highlights of Vatican II* (New York: Paulist, 1999), 162.

7. Philip Roy, *Le Coetus internationalis partum. Un groupe d'opposants au sein du concile Vatican II.* Thèse de doctorat (Québec: Université Laval et Université Lyon III, 2011).

8. Pius X, "Encyclical Letter *Pascendi* (On the Doctrines of the Modernists) [1907]," http://www.vatican.va/holy_father/pius_x/encyclicals/documents/hf_p-x_enc_19070908_pascendi-dominici-gregis_en.html.

9. Pius X, "Motu Proprio *Sacrorum antistitum* [1910]," http://www.vatican.va/holy_father/pius_x/motu_proprio/documents/hf_p-x_motu-proprio_19100901_sacrorum-antistitum_lt.html. An English version can be found at: http://www.papalencyclicals.net/Pius10/p10moath.htm. The oath was replaced by a new Profession of Faith and Oath of Fidelity required of those who hold ecclesiastical office, revised in 1989: Congregation for the Doctrine of the Faith, "Profession of Faith and Oath of Fidelity, (9 January 1989)," *AAS* 81 (1989): 105.

10. See Gabriel Daly and Paul D. Murray, eds., *Ressourcement: A Movement of Renewal in Twentieth Century Catholic Theology* (Oxford: Oxford UP, 2012), and Jürgen Mettepenningen, *Nouvelle théologie—New Theology: Inheritor of Modernism, Precursor of Vatican II* (London: T&T Clark, 2010).

11. *AS* IV/II 781–82; IV/IV 551–53. These interventions are reproduced in Marcel Lefebvre, *J'accuse de concile!* (Martigny, Éditions Saint-Gabriel, 1976), and in *Ils l'ont découronné: Du libéralisme à l'apostasie, la tragédie conciliaire* (Escurolles: Fideliter, 1987).

12. Antonio Bacci and Alfredo Ottaviani, "Breve esame critic del *Novus Ordo Missae,*" *Itineraires:*

Chroniques et documents 67 (1969): 22–24, at 23. I am indebted for this discussion to Gilles Routhier, "The Hermeneutic of Reform as a Task for Theology," *Irish Theological Quarterly* 77 (2012): 219–43; and "L'Herméneutique de Vatican II: Réflexions sur la face cachée d'un débat," *Recherches de sciences religieuses* 100 (2012): 45–63.

13. Bernard Tissier de Mallerais, *Marcel Lefebvre, une vie* (Étampes: Clovis, 2002), 514.

14. For Lefebvre's "Manifesto of 21 November 1974," see http://lacriseintegrist.typepad.fr/weblog/1974/11/manifeste-de-mgr-lefebvre.html; consult this website also for correspondence between Lefebvre and Cardinal Seper, Pope John Paul II, and Cardinal Ratzinger.

15. Gilles Routhier, "The Hermeneutic of Reform as a Task for Theology," 221.

16. Synod of Bishops, "The Final Report," *Origins* 15 (December 19, 1985): 444–50.

17. Joseph Ratzinger, *The Ratzinger Report. An Exclusive Interview on the State of the Church. With Vittorio Messori* (San Francisco: Ignatius Press, 1985).

18. Benedict XVI, "Address of His Holiness Benedict XVI to the Roman Curia offering them his Christmas Greetings (22 December 2005)," http://www.vatican.va/holy_father/benedict_xvi/speeches/2005/december/documents/hf_ben_xvi_spe_20051222_roman-curia_en.html.

19. Gilles Routhier, "L'hermeneutique de Vatican II," 53–55; Cf. "Une magistrale leçon d'herméneutique du concile Vatican II," *Revista Espanõla de Teologia* 72 (2012): 469–87. See also Joseph A. Komonchak,

"Benedict and the Interpretation of Vatican II," *Cristianesimo nella storia* 28 (2007): 323–37; "Novelty in Continuity: Pope Benedict's Interpretation of Vatican II," *America* (February 2, 2009), http://americamagazine.org/issue/684/article /novelty-continuity. See also "The Pope and the Interpretation of the Council," *Commonweal* (July 7, 2007), http://www.commonwealmagazine.org/blog/?p= 1158.

20. Gilles Routhier, "L'herméneutique du Vatican II," 61.

21. Synod of Bishops, "Final Report," 445–46. A similar expression appears in the address of Pope John Paul II to the College of Cardinals on November 9, 1979: "*Mais on ne peut pas non plus courir présomptueusement en avant, vers des manières de vivre, de comprendre et de prêcher la vérité chrétienne, et finalement vers des modes d'être chrétien, prêtre, religieux et religieuse, qui ne s'abritent pas sous l'enseignement intégral du Concile ; intégral, c'est-à-dire entendu à la lumière de toute la sainte Tradition et sur la base du magistère constant de l'Église*" (no. 6) [Nor can one run ahead presumptuously toward ways of living, understanding and preaching Christian truth that do not fall under the integral teaching of the council, that is to say, understood, in the light of holy tradition and on the basis of the constant teaching of the magisterium." (My free translation.) at http://www.vatican.va/holy_father/john_paul_ii/speeches/1979/november/documents/hf_jp-ii_spe_19791106_riunione-plenaria_fr.html.

22. "Mgr Lefebvre et le Vatican sous le pontificat de Jean-Paul II. I. Jusqu'à la mort du cardinal Seper,"

Itinéraires 265 bis (Août 1982). See the extensive citations of this exchange in Gilles Routhier, "L'herméneutique de Vatican II," 56–57. See also, Tissier de Mallerais, *Marcel Lefebvre*, 529.

23. Cardinal Ratzinger did not fail, in a letter of July 20, 1983, to point out the difficulties in Lefebvre's logic, which accepted the magisterium of previous councils and pontificates, yet wished to deny the authority of Vatican II. Routhier, "L'herméneutique de Vatcan II," 57; "The Hermeneutic of Reform," 228–29.

24. Joseph Ratzinger, *The Ratzinger Report*, 35.

25. For a balanced discussion, which draws on the teaching of the council itself, see Gerald O'Collins, "Does Vatican II Represent Continuity or Discontinuity?" *Theological Studies* 73/4 (2012): 768–94. O'Collins notes that the project of Mathew L. Lamb and Matthew Levering, eds., *Vatican II: Renewal within Tradition* (New York: Oxford UP, 2008), "failed to face up to the elements of discontinuity found in the council's 16 documents" (769). Most chapters read like an apologia for the continuity of Vatican II with pre-conciliar tradition.

26. Giuseppe Alberigo, ed., *History of Vatican II*, 5 vols. (Leuven: Peeters, 1995–2006).

27. Augustino Marchetto, *Il Concilio Vaticano II: Contrappunto per la sua storia* (Citta del Vaticano: Vaticana, 2005). English translation: *The Second Vatican Ecumenical Council: A Counterpoint for the History of the Council* (Scranton, PA: University of Scranton Press, 2009).

28. See Camillo Ruini, *Nuovo signi dei tempi: le*

sorti della fede nell'età dei mutamenti (Milano: Mondadori, 2005). On Ruini's presentation, see Sandro Magister, "Vatican II: The Real Untold Story," at http://chiesa.espresso.repubblica.it/articolo/1336648? eng=y.

29. John W. O'Malley, "Vatican II: Did Anything Happen?" *Theological Studies* 67 (2006): 3–33; also in David Schultenover, ed., *Vatican II: Did Anything Happen?* (New York: Continuum, 2007), 52–91, at 56.

30. Stephen Schloesser, "Against Forgetting: Memory, History, Vatican II," *Theological Studies* 67 (2006): 275–319, at 277; also in *Vatican II: Did Anything Happen?*, 92–152, at 93.

31. Giuseppe Alberigo, "Transition to a New Age," in *History of Vatican II*, V: 573–644, at 642–43.

32. Benedict XVI, "Address of His Holiness Benedict XVI to the Roman Curia offering them his Christmas Greetings (22 December 2005)," http://www.vatican.va/holy_father/benedict_xvi/speeches/2005/december/documents/hf_ben_xvi_spe_20051222_roman-curia_en.html.

33. Ibid.

34. Ibid.

35. Ibid.

36. Ibid.

37. Benedict XVI, "Motu Proprio *Summorum Pontificum* [7 July 2007]," http://www.vatican.va/holy_father/benedict_xvi/motu_proprio/documents/hf_ben-xvi_motu-proprio_20070707_summorum-pontificum_en.html.

38. Benedict XVI, "Letter of His Holiness Benedict XVI to the Bishops on the Occasion of the Publication of

the Apostolic Letter *Motu Proprio data Summorum Pontificum*, On the Use of the Roman Liturgy Prior to the Reform of 1970 [7 July 2007]," http://www.vatican.va/holy_father/benedict_xvi/letters/2007/documents/hf_ben-xvi_let_20070707_lettera-vescovi_en.html. For an extensive study, see Chad Glendinning, *Summorum Pontificum and the Use of the Extraordinary Form of the Roman Rite: A Canonical Analysis in Light of the Current Liturgical Law*. Doctoral Dissertation (Ottawa: Saint Paul University, 2010).

39. Benedict XVI, "Motu Proprio *Ecclesiae Unitatem*," http://www.vatican.va/holy_father/benedict_xvi/apost_letters/documents/hf_ben-xvi_apl_20090702_ecclesiae-unitatem_en.html. In response to the uproar this caused, Pope Benedict was impelled to write a surprisingly personal letter to the bishops to explain his action: http://www.vatican.va/ holy_father/benedict_xvi/letters/2009/documents/hf_ben-xvi_let_20090310_remissione-scomunica_en.html. For a fuller discussion, see the Theological Roundtable in: Peter Hünermann, "Excommunication—Communication: An Essay in Layered Analysis" *Horizons* 36 (2009): 285–340.

PART II: PRINCIPLES OF INTERPRETATION

1. For a fuller discussion, see: Raymond E. Brown and Sandra M. Schneiders, "Hermeneutics," *New Jerome Biblical Commentary*. Raymond E. Brown, Joseph A. Fitzmeyer, and Roland E. Murphy, eds. (London: Geoffrey Chapman, 1995), 1146–65.

2. Synod of Bishops, "The Final Report," *Origins* 15 (December 19, 1985): 445–46.

3. For an example of a more organic approach to the key doctrines of Vatican II, see Richard R. Gaillardetz and Catherine E. Clifford, *Keys to the Council: Unlocking the Teaching of Vatican II* (Collegeville, MN: Liturgical Press, 2012).

4. Gilles Routhier, "Vatican II: Relevance and Future," *Theological Studies* 74 (2013): 538.

5. Second Vatican Council, "Pastoral Constitution on the Church in the Modern World (*Gaudium et Spes*)," in *Decrees of the Ecumenical Councils*, 2 vols. Norman P. Tanner, ed. (Washington, DC: Georgetown UP, 1990) II: 1069, n. 1.

6. Gérard Philips, "Deux tendances dans la théologie contemporaine," *Nouvelle Revue Théologique* 85 (1963): 225–38, at 237.

7. Synod of Bishops, "Final Report," 449.

8. Joseph Ratzinger, *Theologische Prinzipienlehre* (München: Wewel, 1982), cited in Lieven Boeve and Gerrard Mannion, eds., *Theological Reader: Mapping a Theological Journey* (New York: Continuum, 2010), 29.

9. Hermann Pottmeyer, "A New Phase in the Reception of Vatican II: Twenty Years of Interpretation of the Council," in *The Reception of Vatican II*, ed. Joseph A. Komonchak (Washington, DC: Catholic University of America Press, 1987), 27–43, at 33.

10. Paul Ricoeur, *Interpretation Theory: Discourse and the Surplus of Meaning* (Fort Worth: Texas Christian University Press, 1976).

11. This principle is enshrined in canon 17 of the *Code of Canon Law* (1983), which states: "Ecclesias-

tical laws must be understood in accord with the proper meaning of the words considered in their text and context. If the meaning remains doubtful and obscure, recourse must be made to parallel places, if there are such, to the purpose and circumstances of the law, and to the mind of the legislator."

12. Ormond Rush, *Still Interpreting Vatican II: Some Hermeneutical Principles* (New York: Paulist, 2004), 1–34.

13. *Acta et documenta Concilio Vaticano II apparando*. Series I: Antepraeparatoria; Series II: Praeparatoria (Vatican City: Typis Polyglottis, 1960); *Acta synodalia sacrocanti concilii oecumenici Vaticani II*. 32 vols (Vatican City: Typis Polyglottis Vaticanis, 1970–1999).

14. The most important of these, given its length and scope, is that of Yves Congar, *My Journal of the Council* (Collegeville, MN: Liturgical Press, 2012); Original version: *Mon journal du concile I et II. Tome I: 1960–1963—Tome II: 1964–1966* (Paris: Cerf, 2002). Henri de Lubac, *Carnets du Concile I et II* (Paris: Cerf, 2007). Sebastien Tromp, *Konzilstagebuch: mit Erläuterungen und Akten aus der Arbeit der Kommission für Glauben und Sitten II. Vatikanisches Konzil Band II/1 und Band II/2 (1962–1963)*. Alexandra von Teuffenbach, ed. (Bautz Verlag, 2011).

15. Ormund Rush, *Still Interpreting Vatican II*, 3.

16. Ibid., 4.

17. The council teaches that "as members of the episcopal college and legitimate successors of the apostles, the individual bishops are bound to be concerned about the whole church" (*LG*, 23). While both the

Bishop of Rome and the college of bishops are said to exercise supreme and universal power in the church, they are not to be understood as separate, competing powers, but as a single subject, as the Bishop of Rome always remains a member of the college, and cannot act apart from it. Nor is the college authorized to act apart from its head, the Bishop of Rome.

18. For a reliable and readable exposition of the principle debates at the council, see John W. O'Malley, *What Happened at Vatican II?* (Cambridge, MA: Belknap, 2008).

19. See Gerald A. McCool, *Nineteenth-Century Scholasticism: The Search for a Unitary Method* (New York: Fordham UP, 1989).

20. On Chenu's critique of the crisis in theology, see Christophe Potworowski, "Dechristianization, Socialization and Incarnation in Marie-Dominique Chenu," *Science et Esprit* 43 (1991): 17–54. De Lubac was also critical of theology's "exile" from contemporary culture. See Joseph A. Komonchak, "Theology and Culture at Mid-Twentieth Century," *Theological Studies* 51 (1990): 589–602.

21. John XXIII, Encyclical Letter *Pacem in Terris*, http://www.vatican.va/holy_father/john_xxiii/encyclicals/documents/hf_j-xxiii_enc_11041963_pacem_en.html, nos. 39–43. The term *signs of the times* first appears in John XXIII's radio address of September 11, 1962. It is taken up by the Pastoral Constitution on the Church in the Modern World, where it is described as a continuing task for the church (*GS*, 4) and in the Decree on Ecumenism, where the rise of the modern ecumenical movement is recognized as such a sign (*UR*, 4).

22. Karl Rahner, "The Basic Theological Interpretation of the Second Vatican Council," and "The Abiding Significance of Vatican II," in *Theological Investigations*, vol. 20 (London: Dartman, Longmann & Todd, 1981), 77–89 and 90–102.

23. See "Aux origines du concile Vatican II," *Nouvelle Revue Théologique* 107 (1985): 3–21; [English translation: "A Plan for the Whole Council," in A. Stacpoole, ed., *Vatican II by those Who Were There* (London: 1986), 88–105.] See also L-J. Suenens, *Souvenirs et espérances* (Paris: Fayard, 1991), 55–131. Mathijs Lamberigts and Leo Declerck, "The Role of Cardinal Léon-Joseph Suenens at Vatican II," in D. Donnelly, J. Famarée, M. Lamberigts, K. Schelkens, eds., *The Belgian Contribution to the Second Vatican Council* (Leuven: Peeters, 2008), 61–217.

24. Joseph Famarée, ed., *Vatican II comme style* (Paris: Cerf, 2012).

25. John W. O'Malley, "Erasmus and Vatican II: Interpreting the Council," *Cristianesimo nella storia: Saggi in onore di Giuseppe Alberigo*, ed. A. Melloni, et al. (Bologna: Il Mulino, 1998), 195–211. See also "Dialogue and the Identity of the Council," a lecture delivered at Georgetown University, October 11, 2012, 20 pp. at http://www.georgetown.edu/OMalley-Dialo gue-and-Identity-of-Council/document/124277346 9086/O'Malley-Dialogue%26Vat2-10-11-12_RE VISED.pdf.

26. John W. O'Malley, "Dialogue and the Identity of the Council," 3.

27. Ibid., 9.

28. John XXIII, "Pope John [Opening Address,

October 11, 1962]," in *Council Daybook: Vatican II*. 3 vols. Floyd Anderson, ed. (National Catholic Welfare Conference, 1965), I: 25–29 at 27.

29. John Henry Newman, *On Consulting the Lay Faithful in Matters of Doctrine*, John Coulson, ed. (London: Sheed & Ward, 1961). Original edition in 1859.

30. See the important reflections on the role of the *sensus fidelium* in the exercise of the authentic teaching office proposed by the Anglican Roman-Catholic International Commission [ARCIC-II], "The Gift of Authority: Authority in the Church III," at http://www .vatican.va/roman_curia/pontifical_councils/chrstuni/ documents/rc_pc_chrstuni_doc_12051999_gift-of- autority_en.html, no. 43.

31. The importance of reception as an expression of the *sensus fidelium* is captured in ARCIC II, *The Gift of Authority*, esp. nos. 24–25, 43 and 50.

PART III: A FEMINIST HERMENEUTIC OF VATICAN II?

1. Betty Friedan, *The Feminine Mystique* (New York: Norton, 2001). Original edition, 1963.

2. Elizabeth Schüssler Fiorenza, *A Discipleship of Equals: A Critical-feminist Ecclesia-logy of Liberation* (New York: Crossroad, 1993); *In Memory of Her: A Feminist-Theological Reconstruction of Christian Origins* (London: SCM, 1994; 2nd rev. ed., 1996).

3. Letty M. Russell, *Church in the Round: Feminist Interpretation of the Church* (Louisville, KY: Westminster/ John Knox, 1993).

4. Massimo Faggioli, *Vatican II: The Battle for Meaning* (New York: Paulist, 2012), 53–59.

5. Elizabeth Schüssler Fiorenza, "Introduction: Feminist Liberation Theology as Critical Sophialogy," in *The Power of Naming: A Conciliar Reader in Feminist Liberation Theology*, ed. Elizabeth Schüssler Fiorenza (Maryknoll, NY: Orbis/London: SCM Press, 1996), xiv. Cited in Massimo Faggiolo, *Vatican II: The Battle for Meaning*, 57.

6. See, for example, Mary E. Hines, "Church: Community for Liberation," in *Freeing Theology: The Essentials of Theology in Feminist Perspective*, Catherine Mowry Lacugna, ed. (New York: Harper Collins, 1993), 161–84. See also, Elisabeth Schüssler Fiorenza, *Discipleship of Equals: A Critical Ekklesia-logy of Liberation* (New York: Crossroad, 1993).

7. Mary Catherine Hilkert, "Experience and Tradition," in *Freeing Theology: The Essentials of Theology in Feminist Perspective*, Catherine Mowry Lacugna, ed. (New York: Harper Collins, 1993), 59–82, at 76.

8. Carmel McEnroy, *Guests in Their Own House: The Women at Vatican II* (New York: Crossroad, 1996). I am indebted to McEnroy for much of the discussion in this chapter. See also: Adriana Valerio, *Madri del concilio: Ventitré donne al Vaticano II* (Roma: Carocci editore, 2012).

9. This observation was made by a Protestant observer, Douglas Horton, *Vatican Diary*, 4 vols. (Philadelphia: United Church Press, 1964–67), III: 165.

10. Of particular importance were the interventions of Cardinal Suenens and Melkite Archbishop George Hakim on October 23 and 24, 1964, respectively.

11. Rosemary Goldie, "Lay Participation in the Work of Vatican II," *Miscellenia Lateranense "Lateranum,"* (1974–75).

12. Carmel McEnroy, *Guests in Their Own House,* 139–44.

13. Ibid., 146–54.

14. An English translation of his speech, delivered October 23, 1964, appears in: "Patrick Keegan," *Council Daybook: Vatican II,* 3 vols. Floyd Anderson, ed. (Washington, DC: National Catholic Welfare Conference, 1965), II: 131–32.

15. Cited in Carmen McEnroy, *Guests in Their Own House,* 145.

16. Cited in Mary Luke Tobin, "Women in the Church Since Vatican II," *America* (November 1, 1986), http://americamagazine.org/issue/100/women-church-vatican-ii.

17. Cited in Carmen McEnroy, *Guests in Their Own House,* 156.

18. Gertrud Heinzelmann, *Wir schweigen nicht länger! Frauen äussern sich zum II Vatikanischen Konzil* (Zürich: Interfeminas-Verlag, 1965).

19. During his pontificate, the Congregation for the Doctrine of the Faith issued a declaration on the question of women's ordination, enlisting the unfortunate argument that only males are suited to "act in the place of Christ." "Declaration *Inter Insignores,* on the Admission of Women to the Ordained Priesthood [1976]," http://www.vatican.va/roman_curia/congregations/cfaith/documents/rc_con_cfaith_doc_19761015_inter-insigniores_en.html.

20. John Paul II, "Apostolic Letter *Ordinatio*

Sacerdotalis, On Reserving the Ordained Priesthood to Men Alone [1994]," http://www.vatican.va/holy_father/john_paul_ii/apost_letters/documents/hf_jp-ii_apl_22051994_ordinatio-sacerdotalis_en.html.

PART IV: A NEW ECCLESIAL CONSCIOUSNESS

1. Gérard Philips, "History of the Constitution," in *Commentary on the Documents of Vatican II*, 5 vols., H. Vorgrimler, ed. (New York: Herder and Herder, 1967–1969), I: 105–37, at 128.

2. John XXIII, "Pope John Convokes Second Vatican Council [*Humanae Salutis*]," in *Council Daybook: Vatican II*, 3 vols., Floyd Anderson, ed. (Washington, DC: National Catholic Welfare Conference, 1966), I: 6–9, at 6.

3. Ibid.

4. Ibid.

5. John XXIII, "Pope John [Opening Address, *Gaudet Mater Ecclesia*]," in *Council Daybook*, I: 25–29, at 26.

6. "Text of Council's Message to the World," in *Council Daybook*, I: 45.

7. Chenu mentions this briefly in his council diary, writing, "The idea came to me that an initial declaration of the council, a 'message' to all men, Christian or not, spelling out the aims and the inspiration of the assembly, in a missionary perspective and recognizing the magnitude of the present circumstances of the world, would effectively respond to the sympathetic expectations of all of those who would be disconcerted if the council got underway immediately by entering

upon theoretical deliberations and the denunciation of erroneous tendencies. This in the style and with the terms of the frequent allocutions of John XXIII, in particular his message of September 11." *Notes quotidiennes au concile* (Paris: Cerf, 1995), 60–61. [My free translation.] He shared it with Congar, who sought out the support of leading cardinals and bishops on 16 or 17 September 1962. See Yves Congar, *My Journal of the Council* (Collegeville, MN: Liturgical Press, 2012), 81.

8. Joseph A. Komonchak, "Modernity and the Construction of Roman Catholicism," *Cristianesimo nella storia* 18 (1997): 353–85, at 356. Also John W. O'Malley, "The Long Nineteenth Century," in *What Happened at Vatican II?* (Cambridge, MA: Belknap, 2008), ch. 1.

9. See Yves Congar, "Une conclusion théologique à l'enquète sur les raisons actuelles de l'incroyance," *la Vie intellectuelle* 37 (1935): 214–49. For this discussion, I am indebted to Christophe Potworowski, "Dechristianisation, Socialization and Incarnation in Marie-Dominique Chenu," *Science et Esprit* XLIII (1991): 17–54.

10. Potworowski, "Dechristianization, Socialization and Incarnation," 26.

11. Ibid., 45–54.

12. "Patrick Keegan," in *Council Daybook: Vatican II, Session 3*, 131–32.

13. John XXIII, "Opening Address," *Council Daybook: Vatican II. Sessions 1–2*, 27.

14. John XXIII, *Il Giornale dell'anima. Soliloqui, nite e diari spirituali*, Edizione critica e annotazione di

Alberto Melloni (Balogna: Istituto per la scienze religiose, 1987), 500. ET: *Journal of a Soul* (Montreal: Palm Publishing, 1965).

15. Paul VI, "Pope Paul [Address to the opening of the Second Session, September 29, 1963]," in *Council Daybook*, I: 144–45, citing Pope John's opening speech.

16. Ibid., 145.

17. M.-D. Chenu, "Una constituzione pastorale della chiesa," in *Do-C*, 205 (1966), reprinted in M.-D. Chenu, *Peuple de Dieu dans le monde* (Paris, 1966), 17. Cited in Giuseppe Alberigo, "Transition to a New Age," *History of Vatican II*, 5 vols., Giuseppe Alberigo and Joseph A. Komonchak, eds. (Leuven: Peeters, 1996–2006), V: 581.

18. "Pope Paul [Address to last General Session of the Council, December 7, 1963]," in *Council Daybook*, III: 361.

PART V: IDENTITY, DIALOGUE, AND REFORM

1. John W. O'Malley, "Vatican II: Did Anything Happen?" *Theological Studies* 67 (2006): 3–33; also in David Schultenover, ed., *Vatican II: Did Anything Happen?* (New York: Continuum, 2007), 52–91, at 79.

2. Paul VI, "Encyclical Letter On the Church, *Ecclesiam Suam*, August 6, 1964," http://www.vati can.va/holy_father/paul_vi/encyclicals/documents/hf_p-vi_enc_06081964_ecclesiam_en.html.

3. See Catherine E. Clifford, "Learning from the Council: A Church in Dialogue," *Theoforum* 44 (2013): 23–42.

4. "Lettre inédite du Cardinal Paul-Émile Léger au

Pape Jean XXIII en août 1962," in *Mémoires de Vatican II*, sous la direction de Brigitte Caulier et Gilles Routhier (Montreal: Fides, 1997), 93–113. See also Gilles Routhier, "Les réactions du Cardinal Leger a la préparation de Vatican II," *Revue de l'histoire de l'Eglise de France* LXXX/204 (1994): 281–302.

5. Also decisive were the interventions of Cardinal Suenens on December 4, 1962: *AS* I/4, 222–24.

6. For the text of their common declaration, see Thomas F. Stransky and John B. Sheerin, eds., *Doing the Truth in Charity* (New York: Paulist, 1981).

7. Paul VI, "Address to the Members of the non-Christian Religions" 3 December 1964, http://www.vatican.va/holy_father/paul_vi/speeches/1964/documents/hf_p-vi_spe_19641203_other-religions_en.html.

8. Paul VI. "Address of the Holy Father Paul VI, October 4, 1964," http://www.vatican.va/holy_father/paul_vi/speeches/1965/documents/hf_p-vi_spe_19651004_sacra-famiglia-new-york_en.html.

9. Paul VI, "*Ecclesiam Suam*," no. 10.

10. Ibid., no. 11.

11. Ibid., no. 51.

12. Ibid., no. 112.

13. Ibid., nos. 70–71.

14. Ibid., nos. 72–73.

15. See Paul VI, Allocution "*In hoc laetamur*," September 14, 1965, *AAS* 57 (1965): 794–804; "Motu Proprio *Apostolica Sollicitudo*," September 15, 1965, *AAS* 57 (1965): 775–80.

16. See *LG* 28 and *PO* 7. The presbyteral council provides a means for the bishop to consult his priests, together with whom they constitute "one priesthood."

Paul VI, "Motu Proprio *Ecclesiae Sanctae*," August 6, 1966, *AAS* 58 (1966): 757–87, I, 15, 1. CIC 495–501; For the College of Consultors, see CIC 502; and Chapter of Canons, CIC 511–14.

17. For an overview of the impressive array activities at the international level aimed at putting the council's teaching into action, see: Edward Idriss Cassidy, *Ecumenism and Interfaith Dialogue: Unitatis Redintegratio, Nostra Aetate* (New York: Paulist, 2005).

18. Bryan T. Froehle and Mary L. Gauthier, *Global Catholicism: Portrait of a World Church* (Maryknoll, NY: Orbis, 2003).

19. Francis, "Address to the Leadership of the Episcopal Conferences of Latin America [July 28, 2013]," http://www.vatican.va/holy_father/francesco/speeches/2013/july/documents/papa-francesco_20130 728_gmg-celam-rio_en.html.

20. See http://www.dici.org/en/multimedia/bernard-fellay-at-the-angelus-press-conference-oct-11-13-2013-part-2/.

21. Richard Gaillardetz, "Francis Wishes to Release Vatican II's Bold Vision from Captivity," *National Catholic Reporter* (September 25, 2013), http://ncron line.org/news/vatican/francis-wishes-release-vatican-iis-bold-vision-captivity.

22. Christoph Theobald, "'L'herméneutique de réforme' implique-t-elle une réforme de l'herméneutique?" *Revue de sciences religieuses* 100 (2012): 65–84, at 74.